EDUCATION AND LIFE

First published 1900
This edition published by Lector House in 2024

ISBN: 978-93-6138-708-1

Lector House LLP
Registered Office: H. No. 96, Block C, Tomar Colony,
Burari, Delhi – 110084, India
info@lectorhouse.com
www.lectorhouse.com

EDUCATION AND LIFE

JAMES HUTCHINS BAKER

2024

LECTOR HOUSE LLP

EDUCATION AND LIFE

PAPERS AND ADDRESSES

BY

JAMES H. BAKER, M.A., LL.D.

PRESIDENT OF THE UNIVERSITY OF COLORADO, AND FORMERLY PRINCIPAL OF THE DENVER HIGH SCHOOL; AUTHOR OF "ELEMENTARY PSYCHOLOGY"

PREFACE.

The papers and addresses constituting this volume were prepared for various occasions. They naturally fall into two groups: papers on Education, and addresses that come under the broader title of Education and Life. The subjects of the first group are arranged in a somewhat logical order, namely: a general view of the field, especially as seen by Plato; secondary education and its relation to the elementary and higher; some principles and problems of the elementary and secondary periods; higher education; the practical bearing of all mental development.

Some of the leading views presented in this book may be expressed in the following propositions: While our educational purpose must remain ideal, all education must be brought in closer touch with the work and the problems of today. For the safety of democracy and the welfare of society, the social aim in the preparation for citizenship must be given more prominence. Although methods that make power are the great need of the schools, mental power without a content of knowledge means nothing; each field of knowledge has its own peculiar value, and, therefore, the choice of studies during the period of general training is not a matter of indifference. Studies belonging to a given period are also good preparation for higher grades of work—a view to be more fully considered by the colleges. In the readjustments of our educational system, the entire time between the first grade and college graduation must be shortened. Some common-sense concepts which have always dwelt in human consciousness, properly kept in view, would often prevent us from wandering in strange pedagogic bypaths. We have suffered from false interpretation of the doctrines of pleasure, pursuit of inclination, punishment by natural consequences, and following lines of least resistance. Evolution and modern psychology, in their latest interpretations, are reaching a safe philosophy for school and life. At the close of this century we have almost a new insight into the doctrine of happiness through work. The heroic, ethical, and æsthetic elements of character are of prime importance. We often find some of the best principles of teaching and rules of life in literature which does not rank as scientific, but contains half-conscious, incidental expression of deep insight into human nature, and in some of the writers referred to in the addresses we find, not only good pedagogics, but fresh hope for both romance and practical philosophy. For our view of life and for our theory of education, we are to interpret evolution and judge the purpose of creation, not by the first struggle of a protozoan for food, but by the last aspiration of man for Heaven.

CONTENTS

Page

EDUCATION.

ELEMENTS OF AN IDEAL LIFE.

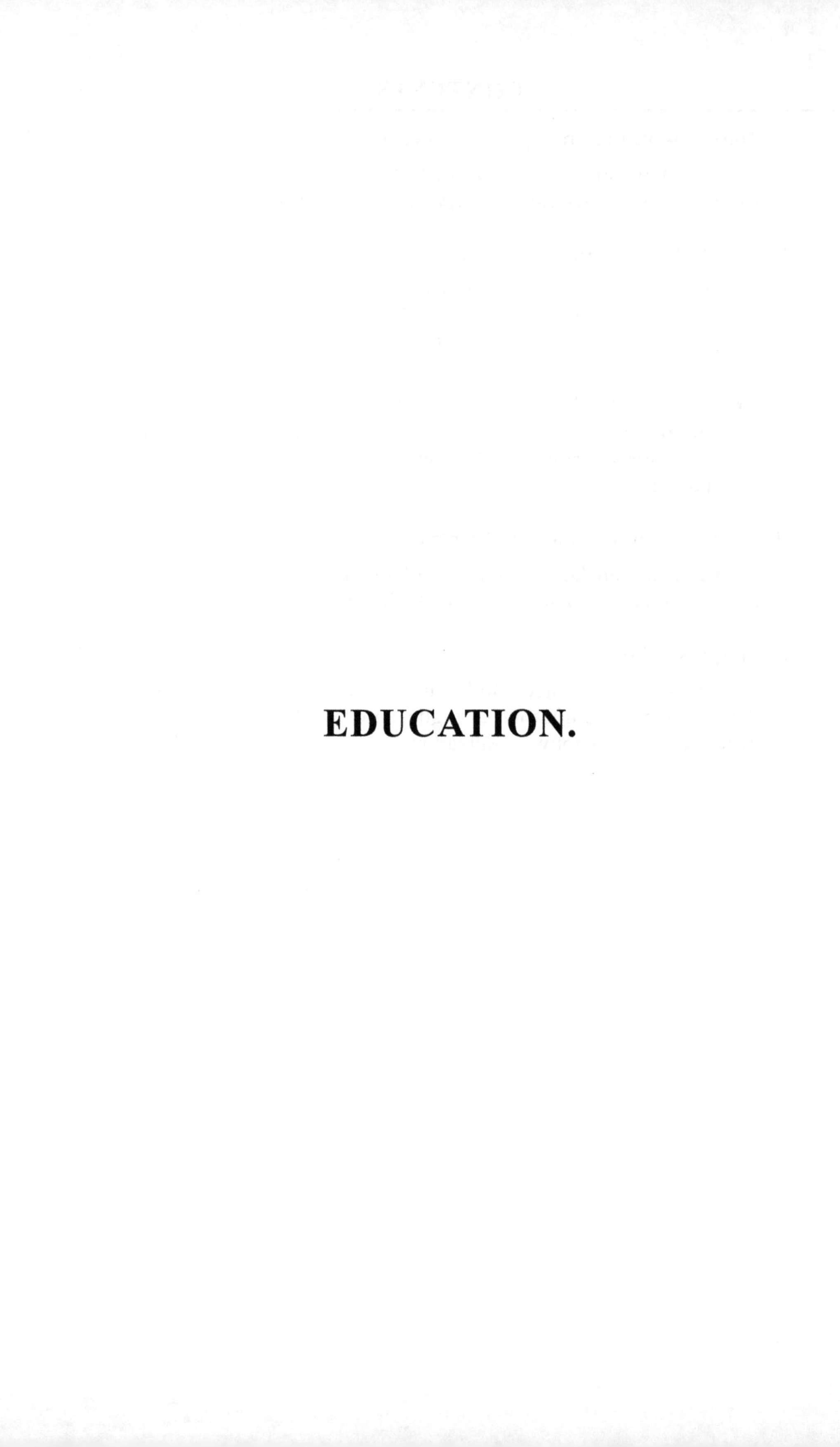

EDUCATION.

I.

HERITAGE OF THE SCHOLAR.

Greek and Teuton—Our heritage—Education—Force of ideas—The material and the spiritual—The American student—Literature of the nineteenth century—Romance not dead—Aspect of science—Practical side.

For a thousand years before the Teuton appeared on the scene of civilization, the sages had been teaching in the agora of Athens and in the groves and gardens of its environs. There profound subjective philosophies were imparted to eager seekers for truth, and in the schools geometry, rhetoric, music, and gymnastics gave to the Attic youth a culture more refined than was ever possessed by any other people. The Athenians were familiar with a literature which, for purity and elegance of style, was never surpassed. The Greeks believed with Plato, that "rhythm and harmony find their way into the secret places of the soul, on which they mightily fasten, bearing grace in their movements, and making the soul graceful of him who is rightly educated." There temples rose with stately column and sculptured frieze, and art fashioned marble in the images of the gods with a transcendent skill that gave an enduring name to many of its devotees.

Meantime our ancestors were wandering westward through the forests of Europe, or were dwelling for a time in thatched huts on some fertile plain, or in some inviting glade or grove. But these children of the forest, almost savages, possessed the genius of progress, a power that turned to its own uses the civilization of the past, and almost wholly determined the character of modern history. They highly esteemed independence and honor. In their estimate of woman they stood above the people of antiquity, and the home was held sacred. They possessed a practical and earnest spirit, an inborn dislike for mere formalism, and a regard for essentials that later developed in scientific discovery and independence of thought. The Teuton had a nature in which ideas took a firm root, and he had a profoundly religious spirit, impressible by great religious truths. He listened to the rustle of the oak leaves in his sacred groves, as did the Greeks at Dodona, and they whispered to him of mysterious powers that manifested themselves through nature. The scalds, the old Teutonic poets, sang in weird runic rhymes of the valorous deeds of their ancestors.

How the Teutons hurled themselves against the barriers of the Roman Empire, how they overran the fields of Italy, how they absorbed and assimilated to their own nature what was best in the civilization of the ancients, how they formed the nuclei of the modern nations, how the renaissance of the ancient literature and art in Italy spread over Western Europe and reached England, and later an offshoot was transplanted to American soil—these and similar themes constitute some of the most interesting portions of history. Not least important is the fact that the Roman world gave the Teutons the religion of Christ, that highest development of faith in things not seen, which, to the mind of many a searcher in rational theology, is a necessary part of a complete plan, to a belief in which we are led by a profoundly contemplative view of nature and human life. We study the past to know the present. Man finds himself only by a broad view of the world and of history, together with a deep insight into his own being. Our present institutions are understood better when viewed historically; in the light of history our present opportunities and obligations assume fuller significance.

By the mingling of two streams, one flowing from the sacred founts of Greece and Rome, the other springing from among the rocks and pines of the German forests, a current of civilization was formed which swept onward and broadened into a placid and powerful river. Let us view the character of the present period, and learn to value what has come down to us from the past—our heritage of institutions and ideas, a heritage derived from the two sources, Greco-Roman and Teutonic.

The independent, practical, investigating energy of the Teutonic character has made this an age of scientific discovery and material progress. The forces of nature are turned to man's uses. Science discovers and proclaims the laws of nature's processes, and evolution admits that, in view of every phenomenon, we are in the presence of an inscrutable energy that orders and sustains all nature's manifestations. The ideas of the Christian religion, universally received by the new peoples, in the course of centuries have forced themselves in their full meaning upon the minds of men, and they determine more than all else the altruistic spirit of the age. Altruism is the soul of Christianity; it has become a forceful and practical idea, and it promises greater changes in political and social conditions than the world has ever seen. The religious revolt of the sixteenth century is a Teutonic inheritance—a revolt which transmitted some evils, but which abjured formalism and based merit upon the essential, conscious attitude of man. If the impulse that grew into the revolution of the eighteenth century and led to political emancipation was not of Teutonic origin, it was received and cherished everywhere by Teutonic peoples, and was carried by them to permanent conclusions. The modern Teuton is found in his highest development in the intelligent American of to-day. The ancient Teuton caught up the torch of civilization, and in the fourteen centuries since has carried it far. It is, perhaps, a return kindly made by fate that the light of that torch was for many years a beacon to benighted Italy. The modern Teuton extends to her the hand of enlightened sympathy, and remembers in gratitude the great gift received from her in the early centuries.

And we inherit from the ancients, those master minds that were the authors of great conceptions when the world was young. Greece was the Shakespeare of the ancient world. It transmuted all that it had received from the nations of the

Orient into forms of surpassing genius, even as the great master of the Elizabethan period of our era turned all that he touched into precious metal. When the world was crude, and there were no great originals to imitate, it meant much to create, and create so perfectly that many of the results have ever since been ideals for all peoples. Phidias and Apelles, Pericles and Demosthenes, Homer and Euripides, Herodotus and Xenophon, Aristides, Socrates and Plato and Aristotle—artists, statesmen, orators, poets, historians, men great and just, philosophers! Can we wonder that the glory of their names increases with time? They were men whom no truly independent worker ever surpassed. No wonder the soil of Greece is sacred, and that men of to-day go back in imagination across the chasm of ages and visit it with reverential spirit. No wonder we still go to the original sources for culture and inspiration. No wonder the great and noble men of Greece are still among the best examples for the instruction of youth. The pass at Thermopylæ, where perished the three hundred, the Parthenon, are hallowed by sacred memories. The Greeks had a marvellous love for nature. They saw it instinct with life, and in fancy beheld some personal power moving in the zephyr, or flowing with the river, or dwelling in the growing tree. Their mythology has become the handmaid of literature. Parnassus, Apollo and the Sacred Nine command almost a belief with our reverence. If the seats on the sacred mount are already filled with the great men of the past, at least we can sit at their feet. The study of the humanities has a peculiar value, because it develops distinctively human possibilities. Thought and language are mysteriously connected. One of the most noted philologists of the age claims that thought without language is impossible. The use of language helps to develop concepts. Fine literature, with its thoughts, its beauty of expression, constructs, as it were, the best channels for original expression. Art strives for perfection, cultivates ideals, refines and ennobles. It creates an understanding of all the ideals that may be included in the categories of the True, the Beautiful, and the Good; hence the interpretation of the aphorism of Goethe, "The beautiful is greater than the good, for it includes the good and adds something to it." Art gives strength to the aspirations, and lends wings to the spirit. The study of the humanities is a grand means of real development.

The present offers the student two sides of education—the modern and the classic, the sciences and the humanities. Ever since the Baconian method was given to the world the interest in science has steadily increased, until now there is danger of neglecting the classic side. Each side of education has its value; either alone makes a one-sided man; let neither be neglected.

In this country to-day the student moves in the vanguard of progress; he is heir to all that is best in the past, and his heritage makes for him opportunities full of promise.

All the soul growth of our ancestors modifies the mechanism of our intellectual processes, and gives us minds that fall into rhythm with the march of ideas. We profit by all the past has done; the active factors in this age of freedom—intellectual, spiritual, and political—are multiplied by millions, and each profits by the efforts of all. Intellectual acquirement is a duty; to be ignorant is to be behind the spirit of the time. There are problems yet to be solved; there are duties to ourselves and the age. Every individual tendency, fitness, and inclination can be met by the diversity of occupations, of knowledge, and of fields of investigation. Men of moral stamina are still needed to stand for all that is best. New ideals are to be created that shall typify an age which yet lacks poetic expression. When we consider the evolution of man and of institutions, we see that we are very far from perfection, and that each period of history is a period of development. We read of the brutal traits of our ancestors, their ignorance, and their superstition, and we can still discover the same tendencies, only more refined and better controlled. Along the avenue of progress we march toward the high destiny of the race. Evolution is the law both of Spencer and of Hegel. Every struggle of an earnest soul gives impetus to the movement.

A Shakespeare, reared on the steppes of Central Asia, among the Tartar hordes of Genghis Khan, would have been a savage—a poetic savage, perhaps, but still a savage—bloodthirsty, restless, and wild. Born of a primitive race, in some sunny clime, he would have looked dreamily upon the world and life, somewhat as an animal of the forest; he would have fed on the spontaneous products of nature, and have reposed under the shadow of his palm tree. Shakespeare of England, by a long process of education, gained the ideas of his age and the culture of the great civilizations of the past. His education and the forceful ideas of a period of thought and reformation and investigation stimulated the distinctively human intelligence, and awakened subjective analysis and poetic fancy, and he made true pictures of human character, world types, in history, tragedy, and comedy. Education enables man to begin real life where the previous age left off. It is an inherited capital. Ideas, fancies, principles, laws, discoveries, experience from failures, which were the work of centuries, are furnished ready at hand as tools for the intellectual workman. The present is understood in the light of history; the methods of investigating nature are transmitted. The growth of the race is epitomized in the individual.

Let us look at the sphere of education. Here is the world of infinite variety, form, and color. The savage looks upon it with superstitious wonder, and, perhaps, with a kind of sensuous enjoyment. He knows not how to wield nature to practical ends. But the book of science is opened to him through education. He learns the secrets of nature's laboratory and, as with magic wand, he marshals the atoms and causes new forms of matter to appear for his uses. He learns the manifestations and transmutations of nature's forces, and he trains them to obey his will and do his work. He observes how, under the influence of a distinct order of forces, organic forms rise on the face of nature and develop into higher and higher classes, and, incidentally, he learns the uses of vegetable products. He knows the laws of number; commodities, structures, and forces are quantitatively estimated, and material progress becomes possible. He traces the history of nations and understands the problems of the present. He catches the inspiration of the geniuses of literature, and he rises to a level with the great minds of the earth; he becomes a creature of ideas, sentiments, aspirations, and ideals, instead of remaining a mere animal. He learns the languages of cultured peoples, and gets at their inner life;

learns their concepts, the polish of their expression, and becomes more enlightened and refined. He studies the subjective side of man, that which is a mirror of all that is objective, and he understands his own powers and possibilities, and the laws of human growth. He studies philosophy, and he stands face to face with the ultimate conceptions of creation and gains a basis for his thought and conduct. This is a practical view, and pertains to the making of a useful and strong man—master over the forces of nature, able to use ideas for practical ends, and capable of continuous growth.

But knowledge as such, and its use for manhood and happiness, are often underestimated. To know the processes and history of inorganic nature, to trace the growth of worlds and know their movements, and number the starry hosts, to study the structure and development of all organic life, to know the infallible laws of mathematics, to live amid the deeds of men of all ages, to imbibe their richest thoughts, to stand in presence of the problems of the infinite, make a mere animal man almost a god, direct him toward the realization of the great possibilities of his being. Imagine a man born in a desert land, and shut in by the walls of a tent from the glories of nature. Imagine him to have matured in body with no thought or language other than pertaining to the needs of physical existence. Imagine him, since we may imagine the impossible, to have a fully developed power for intellectual grasp and emotional life. Then open up to him the beauty of the forest, the poetry of the sea, the grandeur of the mountains, and the sublimity of the starry heavens; let him read the secrets of nature; present to him the writings of men whose lives have been enriched by their own labor, and whose faces radiate an almost divine expression born of good thoughts; reveal to him the glowing concepts that find expression through the chisel or brush of the artist, and give him a view from the summit of philosophy. Would he not look upon nature as a marvellous temple of infinite proportions, adorned with priceless gems and frescoed with master hand? Would he not regard art and thought as divinely inspired? And this picture is hardly overdrawn; such a contrast, only less in degree, lies between the vicious, ignorant boor, given to animal pleasures, and the scholar. Learning draws aside the tent folds and reveals the wonders of the temple. Man must have enjoyment; if not intellectual, then it will be sensuous and degrading. Here is an enjoyment that does not pall, a stimulus that does not react, a gratification that ennobles.

Moreover, education trains the powers through knowledge. The power to observe accurately the world of beauty and wonder; the power to recombine and modify in infinite kaleidoscopic forms the percepts and images of the mind, making possible all progress; the power to elaborate, verify, and generalize; the power to feel the greatness of truth, the rhythms and harmonies of the world and the beauty of its forms; the power to perceive and feel the right; the power to guide one's self in pursuit of the best—these are worth more than mere practical acquisitions and mere knowledge, for they make possible all acquisition and growth and enjoyment.

The thoughtless person who argues against education little knows how much he and all men are indebted to it. The demand for general intelligence is increasing, and the capabilities of the race for knowledge are greater with each educated generation. Earnest men are endeavoring to make a degree of culture almost universal, as is shown by the "Chautauqua Scheme" and the plan of "University Extension." Education adheres less rigidly to the old lines, and men can gain a more purely English training, including scientific preparation for industrial and commercial pursuits. These schemes are useful because they tend to popularize education, and they reach a class which would not be reached by the usual courses of study.

But there is danger of departing from the ideal type of education—education for general training and knowledge and manhood. Not that traditional courses must be rigidly adhered to, for a new field of learning has been opened in which may be acquired a knowledge of material nature. But, in the zeal for the modern side of education, there is danger of neglecting the ancient, the classic side, the humanities. Language and literature, history and philosophy and art, since they train expression and cultivate ideals, and teach the motives of men and the nature and destiny of the human race, since they deal with the spiritual more than with the material, since they belong exclusively to man, since they stimulate the activity of divine powers and instincts, since they are peculiarly useful as mental gymnastics, since they are culturing and refining—they still have and always will have a high value in ideal education. The ancient side and the modern side should fairly share the honors in a college course.

The arguments for so-called practical education are fallacious, whenever the nature, time, and possibilities of the pupil will enable him to develop anything more than the bread-winning capabilities. When one knows the pure mathematics, his knowledge can be applied in the art of bookkeeping with a minimum effort. Bookkeeping is a mere incident in the line of mathematical work. A year in a school of general education, even to the prospective clerk or merchant, should be worth ten times as much as a year spent in the practice of mechanical processes. United States history is valuable to an American youth, but, while with one view America is in the forefront of progress, there is another view in which our century of history is only an incident in the march of events. The present can be understood only historically, and the elements of our civilization should be known in the light of the world's history.

Not only should we adhere to our faith in university education, but we can find reasons for raising the standard of a part of university work. Even now, no student should receive a professional degree who has not previously obtained at least a complete high-school education; and the time may come when, in all institutions, at least two years of college life will be required as a basis for a doctor's or a lawyer's degree. Graduate courses have become a prominent feature of many American universities, and year by year larger numbers of students seek higher degrees. As the race advances, the preparation for active life will necessarily enlarge.

Many know but little of the forces that move the world. Material progress does not make the spirit of the age, but the spirit of the age makes material progress.

The outward works of man are a result of the promptings of the inner spirit. It is the spirit of a nation that wins battles, the spirit of a nation that makes inventions. Take away ideals and the world would be inert. It is spirit that makes the difference between the American soldier fighting for his liberty and the Hessian hireling or the old Italian *condottieri* who played at war for the highest bidder. Here is the difference between a slave and a freeman, between the oppressed of old countries and the free American.

Ideas move the world. It is related that in the second Messenian war the Spartans, obeying the Delphic oracle, sent to Athens for a leader, and the Athenians in contempt sent them a lame schoolmaster. But the schoolmaster had within him the spirit of song, and he so inspired the Spartans that they finally gained the victory. In the contests with England, during the time of the Edwards, the national spirit of Wales was aroused and sustained by the songs of her bards. The Marseillaise Hymn helped to keep alive the fire on the altar of French liberty. It is only as man has hope, aspirations, courage, that he acts, and, in order to progress, he must act towards ideals. The mind imagines higher things to be attained, and endeavor follows.

Natural features of sea or forest or mountain or desert have something to do with the character and ideas of a people; so, also, the material wealth in lands and buildings. But to understand the great movements of history, we must look at the great psychical factors. Our heritage of ideas, our love of liberty, our Puritan standards, our hatred of tyranny, our independence of spirit, are strong characteristics that make us a distinctive and progressive people. It was an idea that gave England her Magna Charta; an idea that made us a free and independent nation; an idea that preserved our Union.

A man makes a labor-saving invention, and the ease and luxury of physical living are increased, and men bless the inventor and proclaim that the practical man alone is of use to the world. Another gives to the world a thought—a great work of art, a song, or a philosophy—and it takes possession of men and becomes an incentive to noble living, and the race has truly progressed. Let the spirit that possesses our people die out and all material prosperity would perish.

In primitive times, when men lived in caves, and, as Charles Lamb humorously says, went to bed early because they had nothing else to do, and grumbled at each other, and, in the absence of candles, were obliged to feel of their comrades' faces to catch the smile of appreciation at their jokes—then, if a great man had a thought, he related it to his neighbor, and his neighbor told it to a friend, and it did good. Later, a great man had a thought, and he wrought it out laboriously on a parchment and loaned it to his neighbor, and he sent it to a friend, and many came, sometimes from far, to read it, and it did more good. In our age a great man had a thought and he printed it in a book, and thousands read it, and it was translated into many tongues, and his words became household words, and the race had taken a step forward. The world advances more rapidly to-day because ideas spread with such facility.

What is called contemptuously "book learning," the education of young men in the schools, helps to preserve, increase, make useful, and transmit all the discoveries and the best thoughts of past generations. The student is likely to be a man of ideas, of ideals, and hence he is the great power of the world.

The man of affairs says to the ideal man: There is nothing of value but railroads, houses, inventions, and creature comforts. Of what use are your history, poetry, philosophy, and stuff? The scholar replies: Every man contributes something to the common good. I am improved by your practical view and skill, and you are unconsciously benefited by my ideas. You live, without knowing it, in an atmosphere of ideas, and the practical men of to-day breathe it in and are inspired and stimulated by it. Without the atmosphere of ideas, your inventions and material progress would not be.

The culture of the ancients directly encourages ideal standards. It was a happy thought of the Greek that personified principles and ideas, that created muses to preside over the forms of literature. Let us deify our best ideals and set up altars for their worship.

Men laugh at the nonsense of poetry and ideal standards, but thoughtful men pity them. I remember listening some years since to a prominent lecturer in a large town. He began with a prelude, in which with masterly strokes he pictured the admirable location of the city, its relation to the environing regions, the whole country, and the world, its probable growth, its material promise, and its opportunity for social, intellectual, and moral development, and he pointed to the picture as an inspiration for young men. Then he entered upon his main theme, "Proofs of Immortality." As with dramatic distinctness he made one point after another, he held his vast audience breathless and spellbound. The next morning I took up my paper at the breakfast table and noted the glaring headlines and details of robberies, murders, and domestic scandals, while, in an obscure corner, expressed in a contemptuous manner, were a dozen lines upon the magnificent oratory and supreme themes of the evening before. Is there not room for the scholar with his ideals?

Rudyard Kipling, that Englishman in a strange oriental garb, visited one of the great and prosperous cities of our country. He was met by a committee of citizens and shown the glory of the town. They gave him the height of their blocks, the cost of their palace hotels, and the extent of their stockyards, expecting him to express wonder and admiration. He surprised them by exclaiming, "Gentlemen, are these things so? Then, indeed, I am sorry for you;" and he called them barbarians, savages, because they gloried in their material possessions, and said nothing of the morals of the city, nothing of her great men, nothing of her government, her charities, and her art. He called them barbarians because they valued their adornments, not for the art in them, but for their cost in dollars. A lecturer not long ago said derisively that of all the Athenians who listened with rapt attention to the orations of Demosthenes, probably not one had a pin or a button for his cloak. It would be a curious problem to weigh a few orations of Demosthenes against pins and buttons. It is said of men of olden time that they conspired to build themselves up into heaven by using materials of earth, and began to erect a lofty tower, but the Almighty, seeing the futility of their endeavor, thwarted their attempt at its inception, and thus showed that men could never ascend to the heavens by any material means. It is a wonderful invention, but no flying machine will ever give wings to the spirit. There is a material and a spiritual side to the world, and the spiritual can never be enhanced by the material. The lower animals, through their instincts, perform material feats often surpassing the skill of man. For his purpose the beaver can build a better dam than man; no skill of man can make honey for the bee. That which distinguishes man is his manhood, his thought, his ideals, his spirituality.

There is a glory of the present and a glory of the past. The glory of the past was its literature, its art, its examples of greatness. Let us retain the glory of the ancient civilization and add to it the marvellous scientific and practical spirit of the present. Then shall we have a civilization surpassing any previous one. Let us not only tunnel our mountains for outlets to our great transcontinental railway systems, but let us also find among our mountain ranges, and domes, and cañons, some sacred grottoes. Let us not only explore our peaks for gold and silver, but find some Parnassus, sacred to the Muses, whom we shall learn to invoke not in vain.

Shall we venture to characterize the American student of the near future? He will hardly be a recluse, nor will he wholly neglect the body for the culture of the mind. He will be a man of the world, a man of business; on the one hand, not disregarding the uses of wealth, and, on the other, not finding material possessions and sensuous enjoyment the better part of life. He will be an influence in politics and in the solution of all social problems. His ideals will be viewed somewhat in the light of their practicality. He will know the laws of mental growth in order to use them, and will find the avenues of approach to men's motives. His religion will add more of work to faith. He will secure a high growth of self by regarding the welfare of others, instead of worshipping exclusively at the shrine of his own development. The scientific knowledge of nature's materials and forces, and the skill to use them, will invite a large class of minds. In brief, the coming student will take on more of the traits of the ideal man of affairs.

But, while we may not expect a revival of the almost romantic life of the early literary clubs of London, there will be many a group devoted to the enjoyment of thought and beauty in literature. If no Socrates shall walk the streets proclaiming his wisdom on the corners, at imminent risk from cable cars and policemen, there will be a philosophy, disseminated through the press of the coming century, which will still strive to reach beyond the processes of nature to the unknown cause, will reëxamine those conceptions of the Absolute, which are thought to stand the test when applied to explain the problems of human life. If no Diogenes shall be found with his lantern at noontide, seeking, as it were, in a microscopic way, the honest man which the brilliant luminary failed to reveal, many a one, living courageously his principles and convictions, will endeavor by precept and example to make an age of honest men who will find the golden rule in the necessities of human intercourse, as well as in the concepts of ethics and the teaching of religion.

The student owes much to the world. The ideal scholar is too intelligent to be prejudiced, one-sided, or superstitious. He should avoid the path of the political demagogue. He should know the force of ideas and the value of ideals; he should be too wise to fall into the slough of pure materialism.

The literature of the future will not try the bold, metaphorical flights of Shakespeare, but there will be a literature that will show the poetry of the new ideas. Whatever philosophy finally becomes the prevalent one, there are certain transcendental conceptions, from which the human mind cannot escape, that will still inspire poetry. There must always be men who will open their eyes to the wonders of the world and of human existence—who must know that any, the commonest, substance is a mystery, the key to which would unlock the secrets of the universe. The beauty of the starry heavens will ever be transcendent; every natural scene and object remains a surpassing work of art; life is filled with tragedy and comedy, and the possibilities of human existence are as sublime as the eternal heights and depths. Such conceptions beget a poetry which rises to a faith above reason; that instinctively looks upon the fact of creation and of existence as sublime and full of promise, and clings to a belief, however vague, in the ultimate grand outcome for the individual. The right view of the world is essentially poetic, and the truest poetry includes faith and reverence. It is the privilege of the earnest and profound scholar to know that literature refines, that philosophy ennobles, that religion purifies, that ideals inspire, and that the world can be explained in its highest meaning only by the conception of a personal God.

Notwithstanding its practical tendencies, this century is not wanting in the highest literary power. It has given us the universal insight and sympathy of Goethe, whose writings Carlyle describes as "A Thousand-voiced Melody of Wisdom." He thus continues, "So did Goethe catch the Music of the Universe, and unfold it into clearness, and, in authentic celestial tones, bring it home to the hearts of men."

This century has revealed the grandeur of metaphysical thought through Hegel, and found a wonderful expounder of science in Spencer. Each an exponent of a great philosophy, both giants in mental grasp, they greatly influence the thought of the age, and become co-workers in the investigation of many-sided truth.

Next stands Carlyle, in the midst of this mechanical and seemingly unpoetic age, and proclaims it an age of romance; in inspired words teaches the beauty of the genuine, the sublimity of creation, the grandeur of human life. Wordsworth, Nature's priest, interprets her forms and moods with finest insight, and finds them expressive of divine thought. He looks quite through material forms and feels

"A sense sublime
Of something far more deeply interfused,
Whose dwelling is the light of setting suns,
And the round ocean and the living air,
And the blue sky, and in the mind of man:
A motion and a spirit, that impels

All thinking things, all objects of all thought,
And rolls through all things."

Our own Emerson to this generation quaintly says, "Hitch your wagon to a star," and thousands strive to rise superior to occupation, rank, and habit into the dignity of manhood—to rise above the clouds of sorrow and disappointment, and bathe in the pure sunlight. The spiritual beauty of his face, the calm dignity of his life will live in the memory of men and add to the force of his writings.

Longfellow has said,

"Look, then, into thine heart, and write."

Every aspiration, every care and sorrow, every mood and sentiment, finds in him a true sympathy; he stands foremost, not as a genius of the intellect, but as a genius of the heart. How often he enters our homes, sits at our firesides, touches the sweetest, tenderest chords of the lyre, awakens the purest aspirations of our being.

Then comes Dickens, and tells us that fiction may have a high and noble mission; that it may teach love, benevolence, and charity; that it may promote cheerfulness and contentment; that it may expose injustice and defend truth and right.

All these, each a master in his field, are powerful in their influence; but beyond this fact is the more significant one that they index some of the better tendencies of the century. Never before were so many fields of thought represented; never did any possess masters of greater skill. We may hope that, even in the midst of this period of material prosperity, invention, and scientific research, the spiritual side of man's nature will ultimately gain new strength, and thought a deeper insight.

With our exact thought and practical energy, is there not danger of losing all the romance which clothes human existence with beauty and hope? The gods are banished from Olympus; Helicon is no longer sacred to the Muses; Egeria has dissolved into a fountain of tears; the Dryads have fled from the sacred oaks; the elves no longer flit in the sunbeams; Odin lies buried beneath the ruins of Walhalla; "Pan is dead." That wealth of imagination which characterized the Greek, enabled him to personify the powers that rolled in the flood or sighed in the breeze, has passed away. We would turn Parnassus into a stone quarry and hew the homes of the Dryads into merchantable lumber. The spear of chivalry is broken in the lists by the implements of the mechanic, the tourney is converted into a fair. Romance is for a time clouded by the smoke of manufactories.

But a seer has arisen, who finds in remotest places and in humblest life the essence of romance. Carlyle is our true poet and we do well to comprehend his meaning. To his mind we have but to paint the meanest object in its actual truth and the picture is a poem. Romance exists in reality. "The thing that *is*, what can be *so* wonderful?" "In our own poor Nineteenth Century ... he has witnessed overhead the infinite deep, with lesser and greater lights, bright-rolling, silent-beaming, hurled forth by the hand of God; around him and under his feet the wonderfullest earth, with her winter snow storms and summer spice airs, and (unaccountablest of all) *himself* standing there. He stood in the lapse of Time; he saw eternity behind him and before him." I cannot lead you to the end of that wonderful passage, but it is worth the devotion of solitude.

We have left the superstitions of the past, but the beauty of mythology is transmuted into the glory of truth. In the valley of Chamounix, Coleridge sang for us a grander hymn than any ancient epic, Wordsworth has read the promise of immortality in a humble flower, science reveals to us the sublimity of creation. Romance has not passed away; if we will but look nature becomes transparent and we see through to Nature's God.

Many good men fear the results of independent thought and scientific research, but such fear is the outgrowth of narrow views. Every pioneer in an unexplored field should be welcomed. The Darwins and the Spencers are doing a grand work. Only the widest investigation can possibly affirm the truth of any belief. Let men doubt their instincts and go forth to seek a foundation for truth. Let them trace the evolution of organized being from the simplest elements. Let them resolve the sun and planets and all the wonderful manifestations of force into nebulæ and heat. Let investigation seek every nook and corner penetrable by human knowledge. All this will but show the processes and the wonders of creation without revealing the cause or end.

The intellect of man, for a time divorced from the warm instincts of his being, sent forth into chill and rayless regions of discovery, having performed its mission, will return and speak to the human soul in startling, welcome accents: Far and wide I have sought a basis for truth and found it not. Any philosophy that recognizes no God is false. Search your inner consciousness. You are yourself God's highest expression of truth. You see beauty in the flower, glory in the heavens. You have human love and sympathy, divine aspirations. Life to you is nothing without aim and hope. Trust your higher instincts.

The ancient Romans read omens in the flight of birds, and ordered great events by these supposed revelations of the deities. In our day, a Bryant has watched by fountain and grove for the revelations of God, and has read in the flight of a "Waterfowl" a deeper augury than any ancient priest, for it relates not to political events, but to an eternal truth, implanted in the breast and confirming the hope of man.

> "There is a power whose care
> Teaches thy way along that pathless coast—
> The desert and illimitable air—
> Lone wandering but not lost.
>
> "Thou'rt gone, the abyss of Heaven
> Hath swallowed up thy form; yet on my heart
> Deeply has sunk the lesson thou hast given,
> And shall not soon depart.
>
> "He who, from zone to zone,
> Guides through the boundless sky thy certain flight,
> In the long way that I must tread alone,

Will lead my steps aright."

The student is asked to take a view from the height to which he has already attained, and catch a glimpse here and there of the world, of history, and of the meaning of human life. The fuller significance of what appears in the fair field of learning will come with maturer years. It is not enough for the student to enjoy selfishly his knowledge and power; he should be a mediator between his capabilities and his opportunities. It is one thing to have power, another to use it. The mighty engine may have within it the potency of great work, but it may stand idle forever unless the proper means are employed to utilize it. Let the student convert his power into active energy, and study the best ways of making it tell for the highest usefulness. Education but prepares to enter the great school of life, and that school should be a means of continuous development towards greater power and higher character, and knowledge and usefulness. Progress is the condition of life; to stand still is to decay. One with a progressive spirit gains a little day by day and year by year, and in the sum of years there will be a large aggregate. Employ well the differentials of time, then integrate, and what is the result?

An old and honored college instructor was accustomed to say, "Education is valuable, but good character is indispensable," and the force of this truth grows upon me with every year of experience. I well remember a sermon by Henry Ward Beecher upon the theme "Upbuilding," in which he spent two hours in an earnest and eloquent appeal, especially to the young, to thrust down the lower nature and cultivate the nobler instincts, and thus evolve to higher planes.

Happy is he who can keep the buoyancy and freshness and hope of early years. The "vision splendid," which appears to the eye of youth, too often may "fade into the light of common day." Too often Wordsworth's lines become a prophecy, but let them be a warning:

"Full soon thy soul shall have her earthly freight,
And custom lie upon thee with a weight,
Heavy as frost, and deep almost as life."

Age should be the time of rich fruition. Not long since the Rev. William R. Alger, on his visit to Denver, after an absence of a dozen years, addressed a congregation of his old friends, and among other things he spoke of his impressions when he first approached these grand mountains. It was at set of sun, and, as he looked away over the plains, he beheld on an elevation a thousand cattle, and in the glory of the departing day they seemed to him like "golden cattle pasturing in the azure and feeding on the blue." Upon his last visit he again approached these scenes at the close of day, and his impressions were as vivid as in earlier years; his enjoyment in life was deeper, his faith was stronger, and his hope brighter. There is no need to grow old in spirit; it is only the dead soul that wholly loses the hope and the joy of youth.

There are three grand categories, not always understood by those who carelessly name them—the True, the Beautiful, and the Good. May the thoughts and deeds which give character to life be such as to fall within this trinity of perfect ideals.

II.

PLATO'S PHILOSOPHY OF EDUCATION AND LIFE.

Historical—Plato and the influence of Platonism—Philosophy—Religion—Ethics—Education, The state—Comments—"Plato, thou reasonest well."

It is the calm judgment of history that, in artistic, literary, and philosophical development, the world shows, relatively, nothing comparable to the Golden Age of Greece. Attica was the Shakespeare of the Ancient World. As the Bard of Avon gathered the material of legend, romance, and history, and crowned the intellectual activity of the Elizabethan Age with results of enduring value, so the leading city of Greece centred in herself many influences of the Orient, and, in a period of great intellectual awakening under favorable conditions, became the genius that produced results of surpassing power and beauty. The Greeks created when European civilization was young, and as yet there was little of the ideal that, in the Attic Period, blossomed into the conceptions of the True, the Beautiful, and the Good.

In any other period never has so great a master as Socrates found so great a pupil as Plato; never has so great a master as Plato encountered so great a pupil as Aristotle. Each pupil grasped and enlarged upon the mighty work of his instructor.

The world still wonders how any age could become so suddenly and highly creative. Like the century plant, the Greek race seemed to have been accumulating, through a long period, power for a quick and startling development. The thoughtful historian enumerates many favoring conditions. The Greeks as a race were active, eager for knowledge, and had a capacity for healthy ideal conceptions. The beneficent climate brought them in contact with nature, and the peculiar charm of their sky, air, mountains, and sea filled them with a sense of wonder and a sense of beauty. We may also mention the stimulus of their intercourse with their own colonies and with other peoples; their religion, which contained the germs of ethical and philosophical thought, and was favorable to freedom of view; the respect for law that sought for the rules of the state and for individual conduct a foundation in permanent principles.

Socrates is a more favorite theme than Plato, partly because he is the first of the three heroic figures that mark the beginning of philosophy. Then his name is surrounded with a halo that was constituted by the events of Athens' greatest period of fame. He lived just after the glory of victory over the Persian invaders had stimulated the Greek pride and every activity that is born of pride and hope. He lived in the period of Athenian supremacy and was contemporary with Phidias, Sophocles, Euripides, Aristophanes, Herodotus, Thucydides, and Pericles.

Plato, on the contrary, beheld the beginning of the misfortunes of Attica and of the decay of Greece. It was the period of the Peloponnesian Wars, of the Spartan and the Theban Supremacy. It was the time of the Thirty Tyrants and of the restored Democracy. But while the time of Plato was not that of the greatest national glory, it permitted the free development of philosophical thought which later culminated in Aristotle.

Socrates, with earnestness of soul, with contempt for the extreme democratic spirit of his time and the growing disregard of divine and human law, with contempt for the Sophists, whose teachings were no higher than prudential preparation for practical life and cultivation of the morals and manners of a Lord Chesterfield, devoted himself to exposing the ignorance and false reasoning of the day and to the search for truth, setting up for his ideal the Supreme Good which included the True and the Beautiful. He, however, was practical in that he taught that all good was good for something; whatever was ideal was to be applied in real life, and he was a notable example of closely following ideals with practical action. "Know thyself" was his maxim, and, in knowing thyself, know the good and follow it.

Socrates is the practical man, Plato the idealist and literary man, Aristotle the scientific man. Socrates left us no writings, and, while Plato in his works uses Socrates as his chief interlocutor, the dialogues are to be regarded as expressing Socrates' philosophy as changed and enlarged by the views of Plato. Xenophon's "Memorabilia" is the source of more nearly accurate views of the life and teachings of Socrates.

Plato uses Socrates' method of induction and exact definition to reach the truth aimed at. Many of the scenes are like plays, some of which would take on a stage setting, with characters that are very much alive and very human. Although in pursuit of the most serious subjects, a dramatic tone runs through the discussions. In the first book of the "Republic," Thrasymachus in argument gets angry, grows red in the face, and fairly roars his views at Socrates, who pretends to be panic-stricken at his looks. Later Thrasymachus asks, "I want to know, Socrates, whether you have a nurse." To Socrates' look of astonished inquiry he more than intimates that the philosopher is too childish to go about unattended. Many of the dialogues are in part historical facts. The characters are the neighbors and friends or intellectual antagonists of the philosopher. The doctrines he combats are doctrines of the day, the scenes are real and in or about Athens. The tyranny he hates and the extreme democracy he satirizes are forms of government whose evils he has observed, and from which he has suffered. You read the dialogues, follow their thought, get into their spirit, and you are brought in touch with the great, throbbing life of the Athenian commonwealth. A few dialogues, carefully read, are worth a hundred volumes of the commentators.

It is related that at a certain time Socrates dreamed he saw a young swan perched on his knee. Soon it gained strength of wing and flew away, singing a sweet song. The next day Plato appeared and became the intimate pupil of Socrates. This is one of many myths, later invented to enlarge the halo of a great name. It was said that Plato was the son of Apollo and that the bees of Hymettus fed him with honey, giving him the power of sweet speech. Myths aside, the chance that made Plato the intimate friend and disciple of Socrates became of vast significance to the future history of philosophy. Plato was of aristocratic parentage; he showed in his youth a poetic temperament, which was later displayed in the dramatic art of his writings. After the death of Socrates in 399 B. C., he travelled and resided at various courts. At the age of forty he returned to Athens and opened his school in the Gymnasium of the Academy, where with one or two intervals he taught for a period of forty years. Aristotle was for twenty years his pupil, and there are many interesting accounts of the relation between pupil and master.

Plato had in him somewhat of the Puritan, while Aristotle was more a man of the world, and we may suppose that he often maintained his opinions with his customary sarcastic smile. He offended the more austere tastes of his master by nicety of dress, care of his shoes, display of finger rings, and a dudish cut of his hair. Contemporaries speak of Plato with admiration for his intellect and reverence for the beauty of his character, which was "elevated in Olympian cheerfulness above the world of change and decay."

In our purpose to touch upon some points of Plato's doctrines, we are treating of a transcendent genius whose work has profoundly affected the thought of the world. Platonism reappears as Neo-Platonism in the second and third centuries of our era; is largely adopted in its new form a century later by St. Augustine, the great expounder of Christianity and teacher of the Middle Ages; arises again in the seventeenth century proclaiming that moral law is written in fixed characters in every rational mind; culminates in the grand idealism of Schelling and Hegel; is transmitted to-day in the magnificent idealistic ethics of such men as Caird, Green, and Bradley; gives the cardinal virtues to Christianity; furnishes a broad and inspiring ethical code for the present; speaks with an inspiration that largely meets the approval of the Christian world; inspired the Utopia and the New Atlantis and all ideal schemes of government and society; was, following Socrates, the father of the inductive method; became the starting point for the scientific study of nature and psychology in the eleventh century; was a large element in the humanistic movement, which at the close of the middle ages created modern natural science; created conceptions which, developing down through the centuries in two diverging lines, indirectly found highest expression in the idealism of Hegel and the evolution of Spencer, and is likely to furnish in broad outlines, especially as presented by Aristotle, ground for the reconciliation of the opposite poles of philosophy in a spiritual evolution.

What was Plato's central idea? It was the existence of fixed principles in the universe, principles realized in the consciousness of man, through pursuit of knowledge. Socrates aimed at a permanent ground for ethical wisdom in a time when the old foundations of conduct and of divine and human law were shaken. He was the progenitor of the inductive method, in that he sought in numerous instances and opinions the essential common ground or principle, and aimed at exact definition. The class concept, general notion, universal truth, was the object of his search. And we find him, for instance, in Plato, tracing through the ten books of the "Republic" the essential character of justice. Plato, following Socrates, sought a foundation for ethical conceptions in a metaphysical theory, the Doctrine of Ideas, a magnificent illustration of the truth that speculative philosophy grows out of man's earnest desire to know why he is here, and what is the meaning of his moral nature.

It will help much any view in the field of philosophy to keep uppermost the thought of distinct classes, types, or kinds of things in nature; the thought of the corresponding class concepts, general notions or universals in the human mind; and the thought of original ideas in the mind of God, as constituting principles or laws or modes of action in nature. This is not a world of chaotic chance, it is a world of rational and progressive order, and we are compelled to seek for the architecture an architect and a plan embodying rational ideas. Plato's ideas are eternal entities existing neither in nature nor in the mind of God, but nevertheless the archetypes, forms, or patterns after which every kind of things to which may be applied a common name was fashioned. Plato here held in an imperfect way the mighty truth of all philosophy, and the "Ideas" have reappeared in many guises,—as the forms or essences of Aristotle, existing only as realized in nature, as ideas in the mind of God, as the self-evolving categories of Hegel, as the perfecting principle and the fashioning laws in the doctrine of evolution.

Man in his preëxistent state dwelt in the region of immaterial ideas and gazed on the fulness of their truth. At his human birth he was made oblivious of his past existence, and growth in wisdom was a gradual realization in the consciousness of the eternal verities formerly known. As in Wordsworth, man's birth was but a "sleep and a forgetting;" growth in knowledge was a remembering. "Trailing clouds of glory do we come from God, who is our home." The truth in this metaphor of philosophy, we may believe, is that man is of divine origin, and hence may know the divine revelations in his own being and in the material world. Here was foreshadowed in rough outlines the spiritual idealism which in its fresh form appears to be gaining new ground to-day. God writes the book of nature; man is the son of God and reads and vaguely understands the meaning of the mighty volume.

Sensations are not knowledge, but the signs of knowledge, as words are the signs of thought, and the mind is innately active and rational, else there could be no interpretation of those signs. This appears to be the true explanation of the fact that we are educated by contact with nature. Without the signs, no communication of knowledge; without the native power of the reader, no reception of knowledge.

Plato held that the ideas were manifest in nature and were also innate in the mind; hence by self-examination and comparison with the copies of the ideas in nature, man arrived at essential truth which was the work of philosophy.

Plato identified the Idea of Ideas with Cause, Mind, the Good or God. God was a personality and supreme above the gods. He was named by his chief attribute, the Good, and of this the True and the Beautiful were qualities. Cousin says, "The True, the Beautiful, and the Good are only revelations of the same Being; that which reveals them to us is reason." "If all perfection belongs to the perfect being, God will possess beauty in its plenitude. The father of the world, of its laws, of its ravishing harmonies, the author of forms, colors, and sounds, he is the principle of beauty in nature. It is he whom we adore without knowing it, under the name of the ideal, when our imagination, borne on from beauties to beauties, calls for a final beauty in which it may find repose." This passage is thoroughly Platonic in spirit and throws much light on the meaning of these absolute ideas of Plato. With change of terms the same passage would apply to Truth and Goodness. We trace them as they appear in the conscious reason and disposition, as they are manifested in the relations of society or are suggested by the reality and beneficence of the world, and we are led to the conception of the perfect ideals whose truth exists in God.

Plato has four principles whose interrelation and process of the active elements determine the world, as the laws of modern evolution are conceived to work out the results discovered by science: (1) unlimited, unformed, or chaotic nature; (2) law, imposing limits and forms upon nature; (3) the resulting, definite types and ideas of a rational world; (4) the Cause which effects these results.

The Good is that which imparts truth to the object and knowledge to the perceiving subject, and is the cause of science and truth; hence, to know the Good is the ethical aim, for to know the Good is to act in harmony with it, and knowledge is virtue.

Plato was fully aware that the philosopher, then as to-day, was regarded by the many as a useless star-gazer, and in the celebrated Allegory of the Cave he shows the relation of true insight to the common view of life and the world. He imagines dwellers in a cave so placed that they see only the shadows of passing objects and hear only the echoes of sounds from the outer world. If released and brought to the full light of the sun they are dazzled and pained, and think they are in a world of false appearance, and believe the realities are the familiar shadows in the cave. After a while they become accustomed to the day and the real objects, and see their truth and beauty. And if they return to the cave, they are half blind and appear ridiculous to the dwellers there. He concludes, "Whether I am right or not, God only knows; but, whether true or false, my opinion is that in the world of knowledge the idea of good appears last of all, and is seen only with an effort; and, when seen, is also inferred to be the universal author of all things beautiful and right, parent of light and lord of light in this world, and the source of truth and reason in the other: this is the first great cause which he, who would act rationally either in public or private life, must behold."

To the Sophist, who follows the opinion of the many instead of regarding fixed principles of truth, he pays his respects with the searching satire of a Carlyle.

His theology, which is a part of his philosophy, has many striking features that have commanded the astonishment of the Christian world. "God the Creator changes not; He deceives not." It is wrong to do good to friends and injure enemies, for the injury of another can be in no case just. If you have a quarrel with any one, become reconciled before you sleep. In heaven is the pattern of the perfect city. All things will work together for good to the just. He advocates the severest abstract piety that, as in the conduct of the sternest Roman or the severest Puritan, swerves not from duty. The myth of Er, the Armenian, reminds us in many points of the judgment day; and his exhortation to pursue the heavenly way that it may be well with us here and hereafter, may be our salvation if we are obedient, is one of the most striking in the history of religious belief.

In the fifth book of the "Laws" is an exhortation to right living that partakes of the spirit of the Christian philosophy. Every man is to honor his own soul with an honor that regards divine good, to value principle higher than life, to place virtue above all gold, to glory in following the better course, to count reverence in children a greater heritage than riches, to regard a contract as a holy thing, to avoid excess of self-love and to adhere to the truth as the beginning of every good. We need no further illustration of the fact that Platonism was naturally welcomed by the early Christian Church.

The ethical ideals of Plato are the most valuable phase of his writings. In the First Book of the "Republic," Thrasymachus, in a dialogue with Socrates, defines justice to be *Sublime Simplicity*, and argues that the unjust are discreet and wise, as some may argue to-day that shrewd dishonesty is commendable. The ethics of Plato is the opposite pole of this philosophy, and as such stands for the rational and moral order of the world. His system is not hedonistic, but ideal. It aims at a good, but the good is attained by a life of virtue.

In a famous passage of the "Republic," the transcendently just man is described. He is to be clothed in justice only. Being the best of men, he is to be esteemed the worst, and so continue to the hour of his death. He is to be bound, scourged, and suffer every kind of evil, and even be crucified; still he is to be just for righteousness' sake. No wonder some Christian fathers believed this referred to Him who was to come, as described in the celebrated chapter of Isaiah. The best man is also the happiest, whether seen or unseen by gods and men. In the "Crito" Socrates will not escape from prison if it is not right, though he suffer death or any other calamity. "Virtue is the health and beauty and well-being of the soul, and vice is the disease and weakness and deformity of the soul." He is a fool who laughs at aught but folly and vice. The possession of the whole world is of no value without the good. No pleasure except that of the wise is quite true and pure. "Is not the noble that which subjects the beast to the man, or rather to the god in man?" "How would a man profit if he received gold and silver on the condition that he was to enslave the noblest part of him to the worst?" "The Holy is loved of God because it is Holy." Not pleasure, but wisdom and knowledge and right opinions and true reasonings are better, both now and forever. The good ruler considers not his own interest, but that of the state. The governing class are to be told that gold and silver they have from God; the divine metal is in them.

Any one who finds in these views a doctrine of pleasure must seek with a prejudiced eye. Plato, as usual, anticipates later ethical discussions, and points to the fact that there is a quality in pleasure; and quality in conduct is the very contention of absolute moralists. He speaks of the soul whose dye of good quality is washed out by pleasure. The attainment of genuine well-being, the development of divine qualities within men, was the aim, and the consciousness of this priceless possession of rational manhood was the incidental reward. His doctrine places before men abstract ideals of Truth, Beauty, and Goodness, which invite the better nature by their supreme excellence.

Plato enumerates four virtues: Wisdom, Courage, Temperance, Justice. Professor Green interprets them in modern form, and maintains their fixed standard of excellence and universal application. Any modern analysis of the principles of conduct which contribute to health of soul and are favorable to success in life, would confirm the enumeration of the Greek virtues. Professor Green says: The Good Will is the will (1) to know what is true and to make what is beautiful; (2) to endure pain and fear; (3) to resist the allurements of pleasure; (4) to take for one's self and to give to others, not what one is inclined to, but what is due. Not only does he enjoin the spirit of justice, but the cultivation of moral courage, and, as contrasted with lazy ignorance, the growth in wisdom which is realization of virtue.

Wisdom played a peculiar and important part in the Greek ethics. Vice was ignorance, because the wise man could but live according to his best knowledge. And the Greeks, properly interpreted, were right. Did we see virtue in all its truth and beauty, and vice in all its deformity, we could but choose the best. Growth in wisdom was a gradual realization in the soul of the heavenly ideas that were the true heritage of man, and in this development the soul was gradually perfected. This beautiful and satisfying philosophy reappears to-day in some of the most ennobling systems of ethics the world has produced. It makes individual and race progress an increase in consciousness of the knowledge of truth and virtue, a revelation of the divine within us.

The Jewish and the Christian conception of divine law as binding man to the performance of his moral obligations was not strongly characteristic of the Greek mind. But responsibility, without which conduct can have no ethical significance, was by no means foreign to Plato's system. In the myth of Er the soul has its choice of the lot of life, and its condition at the end of the earthly career is a requital for the deeds done in the body. Throughout Plato's writings the implications of personal merit or guilt are prominent.

It is a doctrine of virtue rather than of duty. He who sees the right and does not do it is a fool, but that is his matter. He is not bound by any moral law to be wise. If he is virtuous it is well; if not, so much the worse for him. Love of God is the essential of the Christian ethics; knowledge of the Good, of the Greek. To pursue the Good was virtue, and virtue he sets forth in world-wide contrast with vice. Plato's conception of justice, or right, was so exalted that some have thought he attained in later years an insight into the nature of conscience, or the Moral Faculty.

The Greek idea of beauty must be touched in passing. The wise life was a beautiful life. The Beautiful was an attribute of the Deity. They had the love of Beauty which Goethe possessed when he had become fascinated with the study of Greek art, and exclaimed, "The Beautiful is greater than the Good, for it includes the Good, and adds something to it." Plato calls the Beautiful the splendor of the True. The youth should learn to love beautiful forms, first a single form, then all beautiful forms and beauty wherever found; then he will turn to beauty of mind, of institutions and laws, and sciences, and he will gradually draw toward the great sea of beauty, and create and contemplate many fair thoughts, and he will become conscious of absolute beauty, and come near to God, who is transcendent beauty and goodness.

Plato's philosophy makes education a process of developing the power and knowledge latent in the mind, rather than a process of teaching. The Socratic method of *drawing out* is one of time-honored use among pedagogues. Plato defines a good education as "That which gives to the body and to the soul all the beauty and all the perfection of which they are capable." The ideal aim is the harmonious or symmetrical development of the physical, mental, and moral powers. Physical training is for the health of the soul, as well as for the strength and grace of the body. The training of the reason is of first importance. The æsthetic emotions are to be cultivated as a means of moral and religious education. Memory is little emphasized.

The artisans and laborers were simply to learn a trade; the warrior class were to be trained in gymnastics and music. The complete education of the highest class, or the magistrates, was to include music and literature, gymnastics, arithmetic, geometry and astronomy, and finally philosophy. All this was to be supplemented by practical acquaintance with the details of civil and military functions.

Education is the foundation of the state, and in the "Laws" he would make it compulsory. The women are to receive the same training as the men. Children are to be taught to honor their parents and respect their elders. The direction in which education starts a man will determine his future life. In early childhood education is to be made attractive, although to unduly honor the likings of children is to spoil them. The tales which children are permitted to hear must be models of virtuous thought. Harmful tales concerning the gods and heroes are prohibited, but noble traits and deeds of endurance are to be emphasized. Youth should imitate no baseness, but what is temperate, holy, free, and courageous; for "imitations, beginning in early youth, at last sink into the constitution and become a second nature." Children must not be frightened with ghost stories and reference to the infernal world.

Excessive athletics makes men stupid and subject to disease. The kinds of music employed in education must inspire courage, reverence, freedom, and temperance. Art should present true beauty and grace, to draw the soul of childhood into harmony with the beauty of reason. "Rhythm and harmony find their way into the secret places of the soul, making the soul graceful of him who is rightly educated."

Good language and music and grace and rhythm depend on simplicity.

Arithmetic cultivates quickness, and teaches abstract number and necessary truth. Geometry deals with axiomatic knowledge and will draw the soul toward truth. Astronomy compels the mind to look upward. It is to be studied not so much for practical use, as in navigation, but because the mind is purified and illumined thereby. In this connection Plato maintains his position against those who carp at the so-called useless studies.

Plato's ideal state offends the thought of conservative men more than all else in his writings, but it was conceived in view of the highest ideas of virtue and justice. It was simply bad psychology. He enumerates and describes five kinds of states and the corresponding five types of individual character. Indeed he studies justice first in the ideal state, and then in the individual. The three impulses of the soul are compared with the three classes of citizens in the state, and to each he ascribes its excellence, thus forming his list of virtues. But we cannot dwell upon this phase of Plato's teachings. We may, however, refer to his caricature of extreme democracy; it has a useful modern application.

In this state the father descends to his son and fears him, and the son is on a level with his father and does not fear him. The alien is equal to the citizen, and the slave to the master. The master fears and flatters his scholars, and the scholars despise their masters. The young man is on a level with the old, and old men, for fear of seeming morose and authoritative, condescend to the young and are full of pleasantry and gayety. Even the animals in the democracy show the spirit of equality, and the horses and asses march along the streets with all the rights and dignities of freemen, and will run at you if you do not get out of their way, and everything is just ready to burst with liberty. The citizens become sensitive and chafe at authority, and cease to care for the laws. Surely the statesman can turn to Plato for wisdom, for out of this condition grows tyranny.

And, correspondingly, the democratical young man, a kind of *fin de siècle* type, is described. Insolence he terms breeding, and anarchy liberty, and waste magnificence, and impudence courage.

No wonder Plato saw that his ideal state would not be realized *until kings became philosophers*, that is to say—never. Modern dreamers might profit by his wise predictions.

Plato's doctrine is one of ideas and idealism as contrasted with sensations and sensationalism. It is spiritualism as contrasted with materialism. The higher produces the lower, instead of the lower the higher. It is the doctrine that recognizes the rational order of the world, the transcendent nature of conscious man, and his ethical aim. It places ideals before man, in the attaining of which he comes to realization of his true being. It is a doctrine of rational explanation of man's existence. As such it has always strongly invited the adherence of philosophers and Christians. The founders of the church regarded Plato as directly inspired or as having derived inspiration from the Hebrew scriptures.

The doctrine of Universals may be taken with allowance, but we may believe that it represents the right side of philosophical thought. It matters not much whether we hold to the view of Plato's ideas or native truths of the mind developed by experience or the creative activity of the mind in knowing the outer world or the doctrine of participation in the divine nature and divine thought or the power to generalize from the facts of subjective and objective nature, a power above, and not of, material nature—all these views imply man's spiritual and ideal character. Behind man and behind nature is the same reality. In some sense (not the pantheistic, as commonly understood) both are manifestations of that reality. Hence the power of man to know the world, because it is a rational world, and manifestation answers to manifestation, thought to thought. He who claims that all knowledge is founded in sensation is partly right; for to know the outer realm is to realize the inner and to know, in part, the truth of the Universe.

Subjective ideas, in some form, must be retained in philosophy. Our world, as a world of evolution, is orderly and has a progressive plan; hence, according to all human conception, is the product of ideas worked out through what are called the laws of nature.

Men have always asked what is the use of philosophy, and to-day they repeat the question with emphasis. We appreciate the state of mind that rejoices in consciousness of standing on the solid earth, the courageous patience that works out with guarded induction scientific truth, the honesty that will not substitute hasty conjecture for fact, and the faith that works toward results to be fully realized only in the distant future. But many scientific men are coming to regard biological and psychological sciences as great laboratories for philosophy. We may believe the coming problems will be solved by the coöperation of philosophy and science. Science studies the objective side and philosophy the subjective side of the same reality.

Philosophy has a use as an attempt to satisfy the imperative need of men to ask the meaning of their being. It has a use as forming a rational hypothesis concerning a First Cause, and a Final Aim. It is a ground of belief in ideals. All speculative philosophy has been inspired more or less by Platonism, and has given the world the noblest, most hopeful, useful, and influential systems of ethics. Philosophical training gives the power to view comprehensively, connectedly, and logically any group of facts. It contains the presuppositions of science and of our very existence. The investigator in the forest learns many valuable details; if he ascends the mountains, he views the landscape as a whole, and, as it were, finds himself. Finally philosophy represents the supreme, the spiritual, interests of man and aims at essential truth.

Will it be relegated to the shelves of archæology? The signs of to-day appear to answer no. In the whole history of philosophy, the mind has never been able to rest permanently in any extreme or one-sided position or in any position that is inadequate to explain essential facts of existence. Hence it cannot rest permanently in materialism. A recent writer speaks of the history of philosophy as "preëminently a record of remarkable returns of the human intellect to ancient follies and dreams, long since outgrown and supposed to have been consigned to oblivion."

Well! It is strange indeed if nature has evolved a product whose needs, instincts, and native beliefs are a lie, a product without aim or rational ground for existence. If it is so, then pessimism is our philosophy and annihilation our best solution of the problem of conscious life. Most men are too respectful believers in evolution to ascribe to nature any such satanic irony.

At any rate one likes to take an excursion in this field; he feels benefited by the trip. Men still like to seek the great fountain head of philosophy, and take a dip in the Castalian spring—a mental bath of this sort is a good and useful thing. They like to sit in the shady groves of the Academy and listen to Plato or walk with Aristotle in the environs of the Gymnasium. The mighty minds of the past have marked out the broad outlines of truth; it is our work to fill in, to correct. The ethical conceptions were furnished by the ancients. The modern world has merely made them richer in content and broader in application. The deeper meaning of any philosophy or science is learned by the historic method, which gives us the trend of events.

The closing words of the "Republic" are an appropriate ending to the discussion of Plato: "And thus, Glaucon, the tale has been saved and has not perished, and may be our salvation, if we are obedient to the spoken word; and we shall pass safely over the river of Forgetfulness and our soul will not be defiled. Wherefore my counsel is that we hold fast to the heavenly way and follow after justice and virtue always, considering that the soul is immortal and able to endure every sort of good and every sort of evil. Thus shall we live, dear to one another and to the gods, both while remaining here and when, like conquerors in the games who go round to gather gifts, we receive our reward. And it shall be well with us both in this life and in the pilgrimage of a thousand years which we have been reciting."

"Plato, thou reasonest well!—
Else whence this pleasing hope, this fond desire,
This longing after immortality?
* * * * *
'Tis the divinity that stirs within us;
'Tis heaven itself that points out an hereafter,
And intimates eternity to man."

III.

SECONDARY EDUCATION: A REVIEW.[1]

Introductory—Summary of recommendations—Beginning certain studies earlier—The high-school period—Identity of instruction, Better teachers, Postponing final choice of a course—Uniformity—Connection between high schools and colleges, Standard of professional schools, Adequate work for each subject, Reducing number of subjects—Rational choice of subjects—Analysis of the nature and importance of each leading subject of study.

The manner of investigation of the Committee of Ten took a somewhat different turn from what was anticipated when the original report which led to the undertaking was made, but no one now doubts the wisdom of the plan finally adopted. It would be difficult to find groups of men in America better fitted than the members of the conferences appointed by the Committee to discuss the spe-

---

[1] In a report on requirements for admission to college, made to the National Council of Education in 1891, the following recommendation appeared:

"That a committee be appointed by this Council to select a dozen universities and colleges and a dozen high and preparatory schools, to be represented in a convention to consider the problems of secondary and higher education."

In accordance with the recommendation, the committee making the report, of which the writer was chairman, was authorized to call a meeting of representatives of leading educational institutions, at Saratoga in 1892. Invitations were issued and some thirty delegates responded. After a three days' session a plan was formulated, which was adopted by the National Council. The Committee of Ten, thus appointed and charged with the duty of conducting an investigation of secondary-school studies, held its first meeting in New York City in November, 1892, with President Eliot of Harvard University as chairman. The committee arranged for nine subcommittees or conferences, each to consider a principal subject of high-school courses, and submitted to them definite inquiries. Each conference was composed of prominent instructors in the particular subject assigned. The inquiries covered such points as place of beginning the study, time to be given, selection of topics, advisability of difference in treatment for pupils going to college and for those who finish with the high school, methods, etc. The reports of these conferences in printed form, together with a summary of the recommendations, were in the hands of the Committee of Ten at their second meeting in New York, November, 1893. The report of the Committee of Ten, including the conference reports, through the good offices of the Commissioner of Education, was published by the Government.

As a member of the Committee of Ten, the author was invited to review the Report before the Council of Education, at a meeting held in Asbury Park, July, 1894.

cific subjects assigned them; and their recommendations as to choice of matter for secondary schools, the time element, place of studies in the curriculum, and the best methods constitute a most valuable contribution to the educational literature of the period. In the main, they represent the best thought of practical educators.

We shall not enter into a discussion of the details of these conference reports; each report and, in many instances, each section of a report is in itself a large theme. The summary of results and the recommendations of the Committee of Ten will occupy the time allotted.

It was expected that the report as a whole would excite much discussion and invite extensive criticism; and if no other result is attained than the sharpening of wits in controversy, the existence of the report has sufficient warrant.

It is impossible to say of any opinions that they are final, and of any methods that they are the best. Some hold that the eternal verities are to be discovered in the consciousness of the few geniuses, and that obtaining a consensus of opinion is not the way to reach wise conclusions. If we are Hegelian in our philosophy of history, we shall hold to the law of development, shall believe that each stage of thought is a necessary one, that the best light is obtained by the historic method, and that the highest evolution of thought is to be found in the belief and practice of the advanced representatives of any line of investigation. The work of the conferences was to correlate the parts of each subject by the method of applying reason to history; it was the work of the committee proper to correlate these results by the same method. Whether the committee was large and varied enough to represent all sides is to be decided by the discussions of those best fitted to form opinions.

After a careful review of the work of our committee, I venture to make a formal list of opinions presented, most of which, I think, should be heartily indorsed, reserving till later the discussion of a few of them:

1. That work in many secondary-school studies should be begun earlier.

2. That each subject should be made to help every other, as, for example, history should contribute to the study of English, and natural history should be correlated with language, drawing, literature, and geography.

3. That every subject should be taught in the same way, whether in preparation for college or as part of a finishing course.

4. That more highly trained teachers are needed, especially for subjects that are receiving increased attention, as the various sciences and history.

5. That in all scientific subjects, laboratory work should be extended and improved.

6. That for some studies special instructors should be employed to guide the work of teachers in elementary and secondary schools.

7. That all pupils should pursue a given subject in the same way, and to the same extent, as long as they study it at all.

8. That every study should be made a serious subject of instruction, and should

cultivate the pupil's powers of observation, memory, expression, and reasoning.

9. That the choice between the classical course and the Latin-scientific course should be postponed as long as possible, until the taste and power of the pupil have been tested, and he has been able to determine his future aim.

10. That twenty periods per week should be adopted as the standard, providing that five of these periods be given to unprepared work.

11. That parallel programmes should be identical in as many of their parts as possible.

12. That drawing should be largely employed in connection with most of the studies.

13. The omission of industrial and commercial subjects. This is mentioned without comment.

14. That more field work should be required for certain sciences.

15. The desirability of uniformity. Not definitely recommended in the report.

16. That the function of the high schools should be to prepare for the duties of life as well as to fit for college.

17. That colleges and scientific schools should accept any one of the courses of study as preparation for admission.

18. That a good course in English should be required of all pupils entering college.

19. That many teachers should employ various means for better preparation, such as summer schools, special courses of instruction given by college professors, and instruction of school superintendents, principals of high schools, or specially equipped teachers.

20. That the colleges should take a larger interest in secondary and elementary schools.

21. That technological and professional schools should require for admission a complete secondary-school education.

22. That each study pursued should be given continuous time adequate to securing from it good results.

The points of the report which I should question are as follows:

1. That Latin should be begun much earlier than now. (This is a conference recommendation.)

2. That English should be given as much time as Latin. (Conference recommendation.)

3. The large number of science subjects recommended, with loss of adequate time for each.

4. The omission of a careful analysis of the value of each subject, absolute and

relative, preparatory to tabulating courses.

5. The apparent implication that the multiplying of courses is advisable.

6. The implications that the choice of subjects by the pupils may be a matter of comparative indifference—the doctrine of equivalence of studies.

7. Some parts of the model programmes made by the committee.

An examination of tabulated results of the investigations of the conferences will show that in their opinion the following studies should be begun below the high school:

English literature.

German or French.

Elementary algebra and concrete geometry.

Natural phenomena.

Natural history.

Biography and mythology, civil government, and Greek and Roman history.

Physical geography.

There has been much discussion within a few years as to improvements in elementary courses of study, with a growing tendency toward important modifications. Rigid and mechanical methods and an exaggerated notion of thoroughness in every detail have often become a hindrance to the progress of the pupils in elementary schools. The mind of the child is susceptible of a more mature development at the age of fourteen than is usually attained. There are numerous examples of pupils in graded schools, who, with very limited school terms, prepare for the high school at the age of fourteen. Under the guidance of painstaking and intelligent parents or private tutors, children cover, in a very brief time, the studies of the grammar school. All have noted, under favoring conditions, a surprising development, at an early age, in understanding of history, literature, and common phenomena, a growth far beyond that reached at the same age in the schools. These facts simply show the possibilities of the period of elementary education. We understand that ultimately those best prepared to judge must determine the modifications, if any are needed, of the elementary courses. Some say the courses are already overcrowded, it is impossible to add anything. Is it not true, however, that by placing less stress upon a few things, by arousing mental activity through the stimulus of the scientific method, and by improving the skill of the teachers, the work suggested by these conferences may be easily accomplished? All these experiments are already old in many schools in the country.

Consider the logical order of studies. Each child, almost from the dawn of consciousness, recognizes relations of number and space, observes phenomena and draws crude inferences, records in his mind the daily deeds of his associates, and employs language to express his thought, often with large use of imagination. Already has begun the spontaneous development in mathematics, science, history, and literature. Nature points the way and we should follow the direction. These subjects in their various forms should be pursued from the first. Hill's "True Order of Studies" shows that there are some five parallel, upward-running lines representing the divisions of knowledge, and that development may be compared to the encircling, onward movement of a spiral, which, at each turn, cuts off a portion of all the lines. If we accept this view, we must grant that geometry on its concrete side belongs to the earliest period of education; that the observation of natural phenomena with simple inferences will be a most attractive study to the child; that the importance of observation of objects of natural history is foreshadowed by the spontaneous interest taken in them before the school period; that tales of ancient heroes, and the pleasing myths of antiquity, together with the striking characters and incidents of Greek and Roman history, belong to the early period of historic knowledge; that the whole world of substance and phenomena that constitutes our environment should be the subject of study under the head of physiography or physical geography; that the thoughts of literature, ethical and imaginative, appeal readily to the child's mind. We may add that the taste of children may be early cultivated, and that the glory which the child discovers in nature makes possible the art idea and the religious sentiment. The reason for beginning a foreign language early is somewhat independent, but all agree that early study of a living language is desirable.

Should we not reconsider our analysis of the elementary courses? Superintendents and teachers will find the necessary changes not impossible but easy. The sum of all that is recommended for the elementary schools by the conferences is not so formidable as at first appears.

In the conference reports to the Committee of Ten are some views that have a bearing upon the subject of the high-school period. The Latin Conference hopes for a modification of the grammar-school courses, that the high-school course may be begun earlier. The Greek Conference voted that the average age at which pupils enter college should be lowered. The Conference on English was of the opinion that English work during the last two years of the grammar-school course should be in the hands of a special teacher or teachers. The Conference on Modern Languages holds that whenever competent teachers can be secured the grammar school should have an elective course in French or German. The Physics Conference recommended that "Whenever it is possible, special science teachers or superintendents should be appointed to instruct teachers of elementary schools in the methods of teaching natural phenomena." The History Conference thought it desirable that in all schools history should be taught by teachers who have a fondness for historical studies and have paid special attention to effective methods of imparting instruction. One member of the conference was almost ready to advise omitting history from school programmes because of so much rote, text-book teaching.

These opinions are additional evidence of need of modifications in grammar-school work, and some think that ultimately the best solution will be found in extending the high-school period downward to include part of the elementary period.

It was agreed in the Committee of Ten that their task would be less difficult did the high-school period begin, say two years earlier; and the reason why the recommendation of the conferences, that certain studies be introduced below the high school, was viewed with suspicion was the impossibility, with the present organization of the schools, of securing good instruction in these studies.

The following view of the high-school period is expressed by a prominent high-school principal: "My opinion is that it would be much better for our boys and girls to begin their preparation for college at least two years earlier than they now do. If our high schools could receive the pupils at eleven or twelve, instead of fourteen, preparation for college would be completed at sixteen instead of eighteen, as is now generally the case."

The custom in European countries supports the view that high-school methods should reach down into the grades. In Prussia only three years of elementary work precede the gymnasium, and the pupil can enter the gymnasium at the age of nine. The gymnasium itself covers a period of nine years, extending five years below the period of our high schools. Examining the course of the Prussian gymnasium, we find in the first five years, or before the age of fourteen, Latin, Greek, French, history, geometry, natural history; and it is conceded by many educators that more is attained by the age of eighteen in Germany than in this country; that at the age of fourteen in Germany the development of the pupil is more mature, and that in essential features of education he has made more desirable progress.

If our high schools should be made equivalent in length and rank to the Prussian gymnasium, the change would involve the entire reconstruction of our school system, from the primary school to the end of the university. The high schools would become colleges, and the colleges would become high schools, and the graduates from them would enter the university prepared to take up professional or other special university work. That there are many leading educators who advocate these changes for the universities is well known, and there are some strong tendencies toward the German system. On the other hand, many deplore the possibility of losing the American college, which is an institution somewhat peculiar to this country. They think that its broad, general education and superior culture are worth retaining, and that specialization should begin at a late period.

One significant fact stares us in the face, namely, that the average American boy no longer will spend four years beyond the high school in general education, and then pass four years more at the professional school or three years in the graduate course. Somewhere the work must be shortened, in either the elementary school, the high school, or the college.

The whole subject is of great interest and importance, but at the present stage of inquiry no definite conclusions can be reached.

The relation of the mind to a study is determined by the nature of the mind and the nature of the study, and there seems to be no reason in psychology why a college-preparatory subject should be taught differently to one fitting for the duties of life. Besides, it is economy to make identical the work of different courses, as far as possible. There was perfect unanimity in the opinion that the same studies should be pursued by all in the same way, as far as taken.

Every one knows that many teachers are unskilled to present in the elementary schools the beginnings of geometry, science, history, or literature, and that the failures in this work are due to the mechanical efforts of those who have had no higher or special training. The demands of present methods are imperative for improved power in instruction. Science is not well taught in all schools. There is a school which teaches biology from a manual without specimen, microscope, or illustrations. It was a humiliating confession of the committee that the classical course is superior, for the reason that it is difficult to find enough instructors competent to teach modern subjects by modern methods.

A very important point, recognized by the committee, is the advantage of postponing as long as possible the necessity of making a final choice of courses. In this country we have no fixed conditions of rank, and the poor man's son has the same privileges as the sons of position and wealth. Hence, the station in life is not determined by the differentiation in courses at an early period. Very few parents decide upon the final character of the child's instruction much before the beginning of the college period.

For these reasons many would not agree with the conference recommendation to begin Latin at an earlier period. It would not be economy; there is enough else that belongs to the elementary stage of education, and no plan is feasible that is founded upon the foreign view of caste and fixed condition in life.

Uniformity in requirements for admission to college was the subject of the report that finally led to this investigation. Although uniformity is not prominently urged in the report of the Committee of Ten, doubtless the logical outcome of the latter report will be a tendency toward some kind of uniformity. There is a vigorous conflict of opinion to-day as to nationalism and individualism, with a strong tendency, especially in education, toward individualism. In the opinion of many there exists a harmful slavery of the high and preparatory schools to the erratic and varied demands of different colleges, and also a slavery to ignorance and caprice in some schools themselves, which would be removed by a general agreement to uniformity. Men are not enslaved, but are emancipated, by organization, and freedom of the individual is found in the good order of society and government. In a facetious criticism of the committee's report, arguing for extreme individualism in choice of studies, appears the following query: "Please tell us if you and your colleagues on the conference considered any methods for the encouragement of cranks?" No; for the encouragement neither of cranks, nor of crankiness, but for the encouragement of the best kind of rational education. While there are a few wise, independent investigators who need no enforced uniformity, and will not be bound by the recommendations of others, many of the schools are largely imitators, or, worse, are working independently with limited insight, and these schools would be vastly improved by adopting courses and methods growing from a consensus of the best opinions of the country. The lowest would thereby tend to rise to the highest, and from that plane a new advance could be made. Meantime the original thinkers would be free to push forward toward higher results, to be generally adopted later. Through contact of various ideas some principles are settled, and the world is free to move on toward fresh discovery.

The selection of studies is to be determined largely by the nature of the mind and by the universal character of natural and civil environments, and this fact points toward the possibility of uniformity. The period of secondary education is not the period for specializing, and even if it were, there should be some uniformity in differentiation. In the United States there is, broadly speaking, uniformity of tradition, of government, of civilization, and the educated youth of San Francisco bears about the same relation to the world as the educated youth of Boston; hence, so far as elementary and secondary education is pursued, there is no reason why it should not be substantially the same in various schools—not in details belonging to the individual teacher, but in paper requirements and important features of methods.

Nothing in the whole report is more important than the proposed closer connection between high schools and colleges, and this is clearly and forcibly urged. Whatever course of study properly belongs to a secondary school is also a good preparation for higher education, else either secondary or higher education is seriously in error. Whenever a youth decides to take a college course, he should find himself on the road toward it. No one can doubt that in the coming years pupils having pursued properly arranged high-school courses must be admitted to corresponding courses in higher education. The divorcement between higher education and all lower grade work, except the classical, has been a fatal defect in the past. The entire course of education should be a practical interest of college professors, and there should be a hearty coöperation between them and school superintendents and principals in considering all educational problems.

It is a fact of significance that a committee, on which some leading institutions are represented, urges the professional schools of the country to place their standard of admission as high as that of the colleges; and we hope that aid will thus be given the institutions endeavoring to raise the requirements of law, medical, and divinity schools.

The reports of most of the conferences asked for continuous and adequate work for each subject, that it might become a source of discipline and of valuable insight. No doubt part of the work in high schools is too brief and fragmentary to gain from it the best results.

The aim should be to reduce the number of subjects taken by any pupil, and the number of topics under a subject. It is not necessary that the entire landscape be studied in all its parts and details, if a thorough knowledge of the most prominent features is gained.

In one important point I was constrained to differ from the reading of the report, as finally submitted, although the expressions to which exceptions were taken were due rather to the standpoint of the writer of the report than the resolutions of the committee. I refer to those paragraphs in which it is implied that the choice of studies in secondary schools may be a matter of comparative indifference, provided good training is obtained from the subjects chosen. This view makes education formal, without giving due regard to the content. Here are the world of nature and the world of mind. Nature, when its meaning is realized, has the same meaning for all, and in its various phases affects all in substantially the same way. The history of mankind, in its various kinds and degrees of development, has the same content for all. The nature of mind in generic characteristics, and the universal truths that belong to the spiritual world, are the same for all. Mind has the same powers in all human beings. We all know, feel, and will; all persons acquire through attention, retain in memory under the same conditions, obey the same laws of association, reason, so far as rightly, from the same principles, act from motives. Men may be classed crudely according to the motives that will appeal to them. While there are infinite variations in details of men's natures, in power of insight, degree of development, methods of acquisition, predominant motives, in interests and tendencies, all persons in their growth obey the laws of human nature. Hence, we may argue that a science of education is possible; that it is possible to select studies with a view to their universal use in the primary development of the powers, and with the assurance of superior value as revealing to man his entire environment and the nature of his being.

Mere form, mere power, without content, mean nothing. Power is power through knowledge. The very world in which we are to use our power is the world which we must first understand in order to use it. The present is understood, not by the power to read history, but by what history contains. The laws of nature and deductions therefrom are not made available by mere power, but by the power which comes from the knowledge of them. Hence, the education which does not include something of all views of the world, and of the thinking subject, is lacking in data for the wise and effective use of power.

In view of this position, the committee might well analyze carefully the nature and importance of each leading subject, representing a part of the field of knowledge, to the end that a wise correlation of the work of the conferences might be made. The study of number in its concrete form and in its abstract relations, the study of space relations, as founded upon axiomatic truths, are necessary as a basis of many kinds of knowledge, as representing an essential view of the world, as a foundation for the possibilities of commerce and structures, and as furnishing important training in exact reasoning. Science includes many things; but chemistry and physics, which explain the manifestations of force in the material world, biology which reveals important laws of plant and animal life, and physiography, which acquaints us with our entire environment as to location, phenomena, and partial explanation—these are connected with the practical side of civilization and the welfare of humanity, and are a guard against superstition and error; they are indispensable for practice in induction, and they should be well represented in a course of study. History, in which man discovers the meaning of the present and gains wisdom for the future, which is a potent source of ethical thought, must not be omitted. English language, as the means of accurate, vigorous, and beautiful expression, and English literature, which is the treasury of much of the world's best thought, are not subjects to leave to the election of the pupil.

In addition to the training in observation, memory, expression, and inductive reasoning which most studies offer, we must consider the development of imagination, right emotion, and right will. In other words, æsthetic and ethical training is most essential. Secondary schools need not employ formal courses of study to this end, but various means may be employed incidentally. There are a hundred ways in which taste may be cultivated, and literature is one of the best means for developing the art idea. Moral character is developed by right habit, by the right use of the powers in the process of education, by growth in knowledge of ethical principles, by growth of the spirit of reverence, and by the ethical code of religion. All of these means, except the formal use of the last, may be employed by the schools. And the ethical element is inherent in the very nature of right education. To educate rightly is to educate ethically. History, biography, and literature make direct contributions to ethical knowledge.

We now reach the study of foreign classical tongues. If there is nothing more than formal training, for instance, in Latin, the sooner we abandon its study the better. But we find in it also a valuable content. In the process of development some phases of human possibility seem to have been almost fully realized, while the world has continued to develop along other lines. In such cases we must go back and fill our minds with the concepts that belong to the remote period. The Greek and Latin classics give us an insight into the character of ancient peoples and their institutions, give us the concepts of their civilizations, the beauty of their literatures, and make a practical contribution to the knowledge of our own language. From the foreign modern tongues, German may be chosen because of its valuable literature, its contributions to science, its dignity, and its relation to the Anglo-Saxon element of our own language.

We have endeavored to show that the choice of studies is not a matter of indifference, that mathematics, science, history, language and literature, and art and ethics all belong to the period of secondary education; and we have tried to suggest the inference that all should be employed. The relative importance of each cannot be exactly measured, but experience and reason must guide us.

IV.

EDUCATIONAL VALUES.

Criterion—Values—Theory of equivalence—Deviation from ideal courses, Self-activity, Interest, Apperception, Correlation, Coördination, Culture-epochs, Concentration, Laws of association—Pleasure.

We estimate a man's worth by his intellectual grasp, his æsthetic and ethical insight, and his power for action toward right and useful ends. If these characteristics make the ideal man, they should be the ideal aim of education, and a study is to be valued as it best contributes toward developing them. The same test of efficiency is to be applied to the whole curriculum of a school period.

There is a correlation between the field of knowledge and the knowing being. The objective world, with its varied content, answers to the mind with its varied powers. It is through the objective world of nature and of man that the subject comes to a consciousness of himself. Each important phase of the objective world makes a distinct contribution in extent or kind of knowledge to that consciousness. We do not live in a world where cucumbers grow on trees, or where human beings fail in their ever-recurring characteristics; and we believe it possible to discover the kind of value which each source of knowledge may furnish toward the education of the child, with the expectation that we shall not find the choice of studies to be a matter of indifference.

Without laying claim to a best analysis, we may use a customary division of the field of knowledge: (1) mathematical relations, (2) natural phenomena, (3) human action, (4) human thought, (5) æsthetic and ethical qualities. The studies corresponding are (1) mathematics, (2) natural science, (3) history, (4) language and literature, (5) art and ethics. Mathematics treats of quantitative knowledge, furnishes a peculiar intellectual training, and makes possible all commerce, all great structures, and the higher developments of physical science. Natural science acquaints us with the field of physical phenomena and of plant and animal life, is the best training in induction, and is largely the basis of our material civilization. History reveals the individual and our present civilization in the light of all human action, is a source of ethical training, and has high practical value for the problems of government and society. Literature reveals the ideal thought and the speculations of men, gives æsthetic and ethical culture, and in a practical way applies poetry to life. Art and ethics deal with distinct types of knowledge, cultivate the higher emotional powers, and, like ideal literature, set up standards of perfection in execution and in conduct of life.

The world in which we live is the world we are to know in order to adapt ourselves to it in thought, the world we are to know in order to gain power to work therein with success, the world we are to know as representing the thought of the Creator and the correlated nature of man, the world we are to know to gain the soul's highest realization, and, for these ends, to know in its various phases. Each department of study makes its own peculiar contribution to knowledge, each has its peculiar fitness for developing some given power of the mind, each makes its own contribution in preparing the individual for the practical world. In three distinct ways does each subject have a peculiar value—for knowledge, for power, for practical life.

While a classification of studies without cross divisions is impossible, we may say that the first four groups give us the power of knowledge for action; the fifth, the feeling for perfection of action and rightness of action; and these, in their exercise and their tendency, create the right kind of power in action.

Can the exact absolute and relative value of each line of study be determined? No; but we may make approximate estimates through philosophical study of the relation of the mind to the world, through the history of education and the experience of practical teachers. Every position is tentative and subject to constant readjustment, with a closer approach to truth. A reinvestigation of many problems through careful observation of children will doubtless make an important contribution to knowledge of values, if the experiments are conducted with a wisdom that takes them out of the realm of fads, and if the greatest thinkers are not given a seat too far back. Important as this kind of investigation is, extreme advocates may undervalue the store of educational philosophy that has become common property. From Cain and Abel down, the child has always been the observed of all observers; the adult man recognizes the nature of the child in his own nature, and has recollections of many of his first conscious experiences. From the time of the early philosophers, the data have been sufficient to discover universal truths. Child study serves, not so much to establish principles, as to bring the teacher's mind in close sympathy with the life of the child, in order to observe carefully facts for the application of principles.

In an ideal course of general training, can there be, in any exact meaning, an equivalence of studies? As well ask whether one sense can do the work of another sense in revealing the world to the mind. To be sure, the fundamental conceptions of the material world can be obtained through the sense of touch alone; but we also attach importance to the revelations of sight and hearing, and these revelations have a different quality. He who lacks these other senses is defective in sources of soul development. So he who neglects important fields of knowledge lacks something that is peculiar to them. Each study helps every other, and before special training begins each is to be used, up to the time when the student becomes conscious of its meaning. By contact with nature and society, the child, before the school period, gets an all-around education. He distinguishes numerically, observes natural phenomena, notes the deeds of his fellows, gains the thoughts of others, and begins to perceive the qualities of beauty and right. The kindergarten promotes all lines of growth; the primary school continues them. Shall the secondary school be open to broad election? At a time when some educators of strong influence are proclaiming the formal theory of education, that power, without reference to content, is the aim of study, and some universities encourage a wide choice of equivalents in preparation for admission, and the homes yield to the solicitation of pupils to omit difficult subjects, it is important to answer the question in the light of the previous analysis. And we say no, for the simple reasons that not until the secondary period can the meaning of the various departments of knowledge be brought within the conscious understanding, not until then are the various powers developed to a considerable degree of conscious strength, not until then has the natural bent of the student been fairly tested. In this period one would hardly advocate the exclusive study, for instance, of history to the entire neglect of mathematics and physics; nor would he advocate the choice of mathematics to the entire neglect of history and literature.

The question of college electives is to an extent an open one. But it is clear that when general education ends, special education should begin, and that indiscriminate choice of studies without purpose is no substitute, either for a fixed curriculum or for group election in a special line. We may fully approve the freedom of modern university education, but not its license. Its freedom gives the opportunity to choose special and fitting lines of work for a definite purpose; its license leads to evasion and dilettanteism. We hear of a senior who took for his electives Spanish, French, and lectures in music and art, not because they were strong courses in the line of his tastes and tendencies, but because they were the lines of least resistance. There appears to be a reactionary tendency toward a more careful guarding of college electives, together with a shortening of the college course, in order that genuine university work may begin sooner. If this tendency prevails, it will become possible to build all professional and other university courses upon a substantial foundation, and we shall no longer see law and medical students entering for a degree upon the basis of a grammar-school preparation.

The opportunity to specialize, which is the real value of college election, is necessary even for general education. To know all subjects one must know one subject. The deepening of one kind of knowledge deepens all knowledge. The strengthening of power in one direction strengthens the whole man. An education is not complete until one is fairly master of some one subject, which he may employ for enjoyment, for instruction, and for use in the world of practical activity. Here we reach the ultimate consideration on the intellectual side in estimating educational values.

We who are sometimes called conservative know that we have before us new problems or a reconsideration of old problems. We believe the trend of educational thought is right, however some may for a time wander in strange paths. We know that mental capacity, health, time, money, home obligations, proposed occupation, and even deviation from the normal type are all to be considered in planning the education of a pupil. But the deviations from ideal courses and standards should be made with ideals in view, a different proposition from denying the existence or possibility of ideals. We know that the mind is a unit-being and a self-activity, that it develops as a whole, that there are no entities called faculties. But suppose the various psychical activities had never been classified, as they now are, in accordance with the facts of consciousness, the usage of language and literature, and the convenience of psychology, what a herald of fresh progress would he be who would first present mental science in clear groupings! We may call the world one, but it has many phases; the mind is one, but it has many phases; these are more or less correlated, and our theory of educational values stands. We know that interest is the *sine qua non* of success in education, and nothing is more beneficent than the emphasis given this fact to-day. We also know that pleasure is not the only, not even the most valuable, interest; and that the disagreeable character of a study is not always a criterion for its rejection. The pleasure theory will hardly overcome the importance of a symmetrical education.

In regard to some things, however, some of us must be permitted to move slowly. We must use the principle of "apperception," and interpret the new in the light of that which has for a long time been familiar—attach it to the "apperception mass"; we must be indulged in our right to use the "culture-epoch" theory and advance by degrees from the barbaric stage to that of deeper insight; we must "concentrate" (concentre) with established doctrines other doctrines that present large claims, and learn their "correlations" and "coördinations."

A new object or idea must be related to and explained by the knowledge already in mind; it must be so placed and known, or it is not an idea for us. If "apperception" means the act of explaining a new idea by the whole conscious content of the child's mind, then it is the recognized process of all mental growth. In a given study, topics must be arranged in logical order, facts must be so organized as to constitute a consistent whole; important relations with other studies must be noted, and one subject must be made to help another as opportunity arises. If "correlation" means to unite and make clear parts of subjects and subjects by discovery of valuable mutual relations, then it is a vital principle of all good teaching. Studies, while preserving their integrity, must be adjusted to each other in time and sequence so that a harmonious result may be produced. If "coördination" means the harmonious adjustment of the independent functions of departments of study, we recognize it as an old acquaintance.

If the theory of "culture-epochs" finds a parallel, in order of development, between race and individual, and throws light upon the selection of material for each stage of the child's growth, then let the theory be used for all it is worth. Its place, however, will be a subordinate one. Here are the world and the present civilization by means of which the child is to be educated, to which he is to be adjusted. Select subjects with reference to nature as known by modern science, with reference to modern civilization, and the hereditary accumulation of power in the child to acquire modern conceptions.

If "concentration" means subordinating all other subjects of learning to a primary subject, as history or literature, which is to be used as a centre throughout the elementary period, we refuse to give it a place as an important method in education. Intrinsically there is no such thing as a primary centre except the child himself. He possesses native impulses that reach out toward the field of knowledge, and in every direction. It is difficult to imagine a child to be without varied interests. Did you ever see a boy who failed to enumerate his possessions, investigate the interior of his automatic toy, delight in imaginative tales, applaud mock-heroic deeds, and appreciate beautiful objects and right action? If the child lacks normal development and has not the apperceiving mind for the various departments of knowledge, create new centres of apperception and interest, cultivate the neglected and stunted powers. The various distinct aspects of the objective world suggest the selection of studies; the nature of the mind suggests the manner in which the elements of knowledge are to be organized. The parts of a subject must be distinctly known before they are correlated; subjects must be distinctly known before they are viewed in a system of philosophy. Knowledge is not organized by artificial associations, but by observing the well-known laws of classification and reasoning. Moreover, all laws of thought demand that a subject be developed in a definite and continuous way, and that side illustration be employed only for the purpose of clearness. In practice the method of concentration can but violate this principle.

We may ask whether apperception, correlation, coördination, and concentration are anything but a recognition of the laws of association. The laws of association in memory are nothing but the law of acquisition of knowledge, as all good psychology points out. These laws include relations of time, place, likeness, analogy, difference, and cause. Add to these laws logical sequence in the development of a subject, and you have all the principles of the methods named. Have these investigations an important value? Yes. They explain and emphasize pedagogical truths that have been neglected. Having performed their mission and having added to the progress of educational theory, they will give way to new investigations. This is the history of all progress.

The subject of interest deserves a further thought. It goes without saying that all a man thinks, feels, and does centres around his own personality, and, in that sense, is a self-interest. But we are not to infer that, therefore, interest must be pleasure. We are born with native impulses to action, impulses that reach out in benevolence and compassion for the good of others, impulses that reach out toward the truth and beauty and goodness of the world, without regard to pleasure or reward. These impulses tend toward the perfection of our being, and the reward lies in that perfection, the possession of a strong and noble intellectual, æsthetic, and ethical character. The work of the teacher is to invite these better tendencies by presenting to them the proper objects for their exercise in the world of truth, beauty, and right. Interest and action will follow, and, later, the satisfaction that attends right development. Whenever this spontaneous interest does not appear and cannot be invited, the child should face the fact that some things must be, because they are required, and are for his good. When a course of action is obviously the best, and inclination does not lead the way, duty must come to the rescue.

We are not touching this matter as an old ethical controversy, but because it is a vital practical problem of to-day in education, because the pleasure theory is bad philosophy, bad psychology, bad ethics, bad pedagogy, a caricature of man, contrary to our consciousness of the motives of even our ordinary useful acts, a theory that will make a generation of weaklings. Evolution does not claim to show that pleasure is always a criterion of useful action. Herbert Spencer in his "Ethics" says: "In many cases pleasures are not connected with actions which must be performed nor pains with actions which must be avoided, but contrariwise." He postpones the complete coincidence of pleasure with ideal action to the era of perfect moralization. We await the evolutionist's millennium. Much harm as well as much good has been done in the name of Spencer by well-meaning teachers, and much harm has been done in the name of physiological psychologists; we would avoid a misuse of their noble contributions to educational insight. Listen to a view of physiological psychology with reference to the law of habit: "Do every day or two something for no other reason than that you would rather not do it. The man who has daily inured himself to habits of concentrated attention, energetic volition, and self-denial in unnecessary things, will stand like a tower when everything rocks around him and when his softer fellow-mortals are winnowed like chaff in the blast." The fact is, it is impossible to create character, energy, and success without effort that is often painful. This view is an essential part of our theory of educational values.

V.

POWER AS RELATED TO KNOWLEDGE.

Attempt to distinguish between power and knowledge—Illustrations and inferences—Review of article on methods that make power—The recluse and the man of action—Exaggeration of power, Specializing too early, Kind of knowledge important, Specific and general power, Argument for higher education—Power to enjoy, Energy of character.

Try to imagine a material world without force—no cohesion, no resistance, no gravitation, no sound, no light, no sign from the outward world, no active mind to receive a sign. Now try to imagine knowledge without power, a mind that is but a photographic sheet—no active perception, no imagination, no reflection upon ideas, no impulses ending in action. On the other hand, mental power without knowledge is inconceivable. One without knowledge is in the condition of the newly born infant.

As difficult to understand as the relation between matter and force, between spirit and body, between thought and its sign, is the relation between knowledge and power. In a way we may attempt to separate and distinguish between them, by a process of emphasizing the one or the other. Knowledge, in the sense of information, means an acquaintance with nature in its infinite variety of kind, form, and color, and with man in history and literature; mental power is the ability to gain knowledge, and the motive to use it for growth and for valuable ends. Mere knowledge serenely contemplates nature and history as a panorama, without serious reflection or effort. Power is able to reflect upon knowledge, and to find motives for progress and useful action. Knowledge is the product of the information method; power, of the method of self-activity.

As we cannot divorce matter and force, so it appears we cannot clearly separate knowledge and mental power; the distinction is artificial and almost fanciful. The one cannot exist without the other; they are the opposite sides of the shield. Through knowledge comes power. Knowledge is the material for reflection and action. Knowledge, as it were, creates the mind, and is both the source of power and the occasion for its use.

We recall the familiar caricature of the Chinese lack of original power. A merchant negotiated with a Chinaman for the manufacture of a few thousand plates of a certain pattern, and furnished a sample that by chance was cracked. The plates arrived in due season, admirably imitating the original—and every one was cracked. No need in this instance to employ the mandate given by a choleric superintendent to an employee, who on one occasion thought for himself—"I have told you repeatedly you have no business to think!" The Chinese character may be expressed by a parody on a familiar stanza:

> For they are the same their fathers have been;
> They see the same sights their fathers have seen,
> They drink the same stream and view the same sun,
> And run the same course their fathers have run.

A timorous cow gazing wistfully over the garden gate at the forbidden succulent vegetables, and nervously rubbing her nose by accident against the latch, may open the gate and gain an entrance, and afterward repeat the process. A new and peculiar fastening will prevent any further depredations. An ingenious boy will find the means to undo any kind of unique fastening to the gate that bars him from the watermelon patch. Charles Lamb humorously describes how the Chinese learned to eat roast pig. A house burned and the family pig perished in the flames; a disconsolate group of people stood around viewing the ruins, when by accident one touched the pig and, burning his finger, thrust it in his mouth to cool it; the taste was good, and he repeated the process. Soon there were marvellously frequent conflagrations—all the neighbors burned their houses to roast their pigs, that being the only method they had learned.

From these somewhat trivial illustrations, we may readily draw a few inferences: First, ingenuity of mind for novel conditions distinguishes man from the brutes; second, the Chinese method of education emphasizes too much the information side—it is not good; third, the human mind is ingenious when it is rightly educated and has a strong motive; fourth, ingenuity is the power that should grow from education. In this idea—ingenuity of mind—is the very essence of what we mean when we emphasize the power side of the soul.

The problem of education is to make men think. Tradition, authority, formalism have not the place in education which they formerly occupied. May it not be that we have so analyzed and formulated the work of the schools that formalism and method have somewhat taken the place of genuine work, full of the life and spirit that make power? We may discover that the criticisms from certain high sources have an element of truth in them. A certain routine may easily become a sacred code, a law of the tables, and any variation therefrom an impiety.

A person possesses power when his conception ploughs through the unfurrowed tissue of his brain to seek its proper affinity, and unites with it to form a correct judgment. A person who is merely instructed does not construct new lines of thought to bring ideas into novel relations; he does not originate or progress. An original thinker masses all congruous ideas around a dimly conceived notion and there is a new birth of an idea, a genuine child of the brain. His ingenuity will open a gate or construct a philosophical system.

Every student remembers well the stages in his education when there was a new awakening by methods that invited thought, when a power was gained to conceive and do something not stated in the books or imparted by the teacher. In the schools, even of to-day, teachers are not always found who can impart elementary science in the spirit of science, who can successfully invite speculation as to causes, who can teach accurate perception, who can interpret events in history, train pupils in the use of reference books, or invite original thought in mathematics. There is no high school which does not yearly receive pupils not trained in original power, no college which does not annually winnow out freshmen, because they have not gained the power to grapple with virile methods. The defect is sometimes innate, but it is oftener due to false methods of instruction. Our great problem is to make scholars who are not hopeless and helpless in the presence of what they have not learned.

The plant must have good soil, water and air and sun, care and pruning, in order to grow, but it grows of itself, gains strength by proper nourishment. The aggregation of material about the plant does not constitute its growth. The plant must assimilate; the juices of life must flow through it.

The teacher does his best work when he makes all conditions favorable for the self-activity of the pupil. Such conditions create a lively interest in the objects and forces of nature, invite examination of facts and discovery of relations, arouse the imagination to conceive results, awaken query and reflection, stimulate the emotional life toward worthy and energetic action, and make the pupil ever progressive.

An article in one of our magazines strongly emphasizes the methods that make power. It considers the kind of training that finally makes accurate thinkers, that makes original, progressive men, men of power, and safe and wise citizens. The author shows that clear observation, accurate recording of facts, just inference, and strong, choice expression are most important ends to be attained by the work of the schools, and that these ends become the means for correcting all sorts of unjust, illogical conclusions as to politics and morals.

There is much profound thought in the view maintained. Unjust inferences, fallacies, are nearly the sum of the world's social and political evils. False ideas are held as true concerning all sorts of current problems—notions that take possession of men's minds without logical reflection. The fallacy of confounding sequence with cause is almost universal. All kinds of subjective and objective duties suffer from illogical minds.

To correct many errors and evils, to make thinking, useful men, we must emphasize the processes recommended: (1) observation, (2) faithful recording, (3) just inference, (4) satisfactory expression.

The author shows wherein the work of the grades fails to give the desired results. He holds that arithmetic, so emphasized, contributes nothing because it employs necessary reasoning, and does not give practice in inference from observation and experience, a process which develops scientific judgment. Inductive reasoning alone can give scientific power. Reading, writing, spelling, geography as usually taught, contribute but little; grammar does not add much.

For invention, for correct estimates of the problems of society, government, and morals, the original power of inference from observed facts is necessary. It is asked: Do our schools give this power to a satisfactory and attainable degree? It is claimed in the article that the high schools and colleges fail more or less, because so much time is given to memory work and formulated results. In the high schools the work to be most emphasized is not chosen with discrimination. The courses include too many studies, not well done. There should be fewer studies so pursued as to give power.

May it not be well to make the inquiry in all grades as to what proportion of the work contributes toward the final result of accurate reflection upon the world of facts. Let us again repeat the author's list in logical order: (1) observation, (2) recording, as in noting experiments, (3) inference, (4) expression.

President Eliot's paper here referred to admirably emphasizes the methods that make power. Perhaps the author gives too little importance to knowledge as the basis of power, and fails to emphasize the æsthetic power and the value of ideals. It is true that poetry implies accurate observation, fine discrimination, discovery of just relations, and true insight, but it is equally true that science study does not make poets.

The times have changed. The old idea of the scholar was of one who, in the serene contemplation of truth, beauty, and goodness, found a never-failing source of delight for himself, and felt little obligation to the world that sustained him, or the social environment that nurtured and humanized him. The devotion to truth for its own sake, the love of nature in repose, the admiration of great deeds, fine sentiments and noble thoughts, were for him sufficient, as if he were isolated in a world of his own. We do not depreciate such interest, for life is worth nothing without it. But there is a demand for action, a call to externalize the power of one's being. Each man is a part of the all, from eternity destined to be a factor in the progress of all. The thoughts and impulses that evaporate and accomplish nothing are not of much more value to the individual than to his neighbor. "Do something" is the command alike of religion and of the nature of our physical being. Every sentiment and idea that leads to action forms a habit in the mysterious inner chambers of our nervous system for action, and we gain in power, grow in mental stature, day by day.

Power comes through knowledge. There may be too great a tendency to emphasize power to the loss of that knowledge necessary to marshal in one field of view the necessary facts. Imagine a judge trying to reach a decision without the points in evidence before his mind; a statesman that would interpret current events without a knowledge of history; an investigator in science who had not before him the results of the investigations of others.

Ideally, knowledge should be varied and comprehensive; it should cover, at least in an elementary way, the entire field of nature and of man. Then only is the student best prepared for his life work, if he would make the most of it. A man lost in a forest directs not his steps wisely; when thoroughly acquainted with his surroundings, he moves forward with confidence. One who has trained all the muscles of his body delivers a blow with vigor. One who has trained all the powers of his mind summons to his aid the energy of all, when he acts in a given direction. His knowledge is the light thrown on his endeavor.

This view is opposed to the extreme doctrine that knowledge is of little value. Knowledge is necessary to power; the abuse lies in not making it the basis of power.

This theory also militates strongly against the position that a student should specialize at too early a period, before he has traversed in an elementary way the circle of studies and gained a harmonized general development.

The discussion of a growing fallacy naturally appears in this place, that it makes no difference what knowledge is used provided it gives power. It does make a difference whether one gains power in deciphering an ancient inscription in hieroglyphics, or gains it by studying a language which contains the generic concepts of our native tongue, or in pursuing a scientific study which acquaints him with the laws of nature's forces. In the one case, while the power is great, the knowledge is small; in the other, an essential view of the thought of mankind or of the nature of the world in which we live is gained, and the knowledge is broadly useful for various exercise of power.

Another fallacy is the doctrine that actual execution in practical ways alone gives power. It may give ready specific power of a limited kind, but it may leave the man childlike and helpless in the presence of anything but his specialty.

Here we find an argument for higher education, for an accumulation of knowledge and power that comes through prolonged labor in the field of learning, under wise guidance and through self-effort. Many a youth, through limited capacity, limited time and means, must begin special education before he has laid a broad foundation, but this is not the ideal method. The true teacher will always hold the highest ideals before the pupils, will guide them in the path of general education, until that education becomes what is called liberal. The broad-minded men who conduct schools for special education are strong advocates of the highest degree of general training as a foundation.

Four years of college life, with the methods of to-day, more than quadruple the capital of the graduate of the secondary school. They broaden the field of knowledge, and enlarge the capacity for doing. The world is full of demands for men of knowledge and power. There is to-day a lack of men sufficiently equipped in knowledge, power, and character to take the direction, for instance, of important college departments. Men of power and skill are in demand everywhere, and not enough can be found for responsible positions. One half the fault is insufficient education.

There is another phase of power that must not be neglected, the power to enjoy, to be rich in emotional life. Knowledge, properly pursued, is a source of rich and refined intellectual emotions. There is joy in discovery, joy in the freedom and grasp of thought.

Æsthetic power, based upon fine discrimination, finds a perpetual joy in sky and sea, and mountain and forest, in music and poetry, in sentiment and song. Our Teutonic ancestors were better seers than we. The morning sun and the midnight darkness were perpetually to them a new birth. The leaves whispered to them divine messages; the storms and the seasons, the fruitful earth, were full of wonder and sacred mysteries. They were poets. This matter-of-fact age will yet return to the primitive regard for nature, a regard enlightened and refined by science. Men will yet find in the most commonplace fact of nature mystery, poetry, ground for reverence, and faith in a God.

The power of enjoyment alone does not give a fruitful life. It is in the moment of action that we gain the habit that makes power for action. As a philosopher recently expressed it: Do not allow your finer emotions to evaporate without finding expression in some useful act, if it is nothing but speaking kindly to your grandmother, or giving up your seat in a horse car.

There has been a weak and harmful philosophy in vogue for years that would place the natural and the useful in the line of the agreeable. Even extreme evolution fails signally to show that the agreeable is always teleological, that is, always directed toward useful ends. The latest teaching of physiological psychology takes us back to the stern philosophy of the self-denying Puritan, and shows that we must conquer our habitual inclinations, and encounter some disagreeable duty every day to prepare for the emergencies that demand men of stern stuff. George Eliot proclaims the same thought with philosophical insight, that we are not to wait for great opportunities for glory, but by daily, drudging performance of little duties are to get ready for the arrival of the great opportunities. We must prepare for our eagle flights by many feeble attempts of our untried pinions.

If one but work, no matter in what line of higher scholastic pursuit, he will in a few years waken to a consciousness of power that makes him one of the leaders. There is every encouragement to the student to persevere, in the certain assurance that sooner or later he will reach attainments beyond his present clear conception.

Our inheritance is a glorious one. The character of the Anglo-Saxons is seen throughout their history. Amid the clash of weapons they fought with a fierce energy and a strange delight. They rode the mighty billows and sang heroic songs with the wild joy of the sea fowl. Later we find them contending earnestly for their beliefs. Then they grew into the Puritan sternness of character, abounding in the sense of duty. Their character has made them the leaders and conquerors of the world. It finds expression in the progress and influence of America. This energy has gradually become more and more refined and humanized, and, in its highest and best form, it is the heritage of every young man; and by the pride of ancestry, by the character inherited, by the opportunity of his age, he is called upon to wield strongly the weapon of Thor and hammer out his destiny with strong heart and earnest purpose.

VI.

MORAL TRAINING.

Introductory—Habit—Leadership—Historic examples, Literature—Precept, Objects for activity—Duty—What the schools are doing.

We shall not discuss the philosophical systems which underlie ethical theories, nor the theories themselves which consider the nature of the moral sense and the supreme aim of life, but shall treat practical ethics as a part of didactics, and as a part of that unspoken influence which should be the constant ally of instruction. It is not the purpose to present anything new, but rather to give confidence in methods that are well known and are successfully employed by skilful and devoted teachers.

The formation of right habits is the first step toward good character. Aristotle gives this fact special emphasis. Here are some detached sentences from his ethics: "Moral virtue is the outcome of habit, and, accordingly, its name is derived by a slight deflection from habit.... It is by playing the harp that both good and bad harpists are produced, and the case of builders and all *artisans* is similar, as it is by building well that they will be good builders, and by building badly that they will be bad builders.... Accordingly, the difference between one training of the habits and another, from early days, is not a light matter, but is serious or all-important." Aristotle here expresses a truth that has become one of the tritest. All mental dispositions are strengthened by repetition. We learn to observe by observing, to remember by exercising memory, to create by training the imagination, to reason by acts of inference. Passions grow by indulgence and diminish by restraint; the finer emotions gain strength by use. Courage, endurance, firmness are established by frequently facing dangers and difficulties. By practice, disagreeable acts may become a pleasure.

It is by practice that the mind gets possession of the body, that the separate movements of the child become correlated, and the most complex acts are performed with ease and accuracy. Physiological psychology has confirmed and strengthened the doctrine of habit. The functions of the brain and mental actions are correlated. A nerve tract once established in the brain, and action along that line recurs with increasing spontaneity. New lines of communication are formed with difficulty. Each physical act controlled by lower nerve centres leaves a tendency in those centres to repeat the act.

The inference is obvious and important. Whatever we wish the adult man to be, we must help him to become by early practice. Childhood is the period when tendencies are most easily established. The mind is teachable and receives impressions readily; around those cluster kindred impressions, and the formation of character is already begun. The brain and other nerve centres are plastic, and readily act in any manner not inconsistent with their natural functions. As they begin they tend to act thereafter.

Dr. Harris called attention a few years ago to the ethical import of the ordinary requirements and prohibitions of the schoolroom. Promptness, obedience, silence, respect, right positions in sitting and standing, regard for the rights of others, were named as helping to form habits that would make the child self-controlled and fit him to live in society.

Whatever you would wish the child to do and become, that let him practise. We learn to do, not by knowing, but by knowing and then doing. Ethical teaching, tales of heroic deeds, soul-stirring fiction that awakens sympathetic emotions may accomplish but little, unless in the child's early life regard for the right, little acts of heroism, and deeds of sympathy are employed; unless the ideas and feeling find expression in action, and so become a part of the child's power and tendency. George Eliot would have us make ready for great deeds by constant performance of little duties at hand.

Right habit is the only sure foundation for character. Sudden resolutions to change the tenor of life, sudden conversion from an evil life to one of ideal goodness are usually failures, because the old tendencies will hold on grimly until the new impulse, however great, has gradually evaporated. To prepare for the highest moral life and a persevering religious life, early habits of the right kind are the only secure foundation.

The teacher may have confidence in the value of requiring of pupils practice in self-restraint, practice in encountering difficulties that demand a little of courage, a little even of heroism—and each day furnishes opportunities. Pleasure may not always attend their efforts, but pleasure will come soon enough as a reward, in consciousness of strength and of noble development. Often we do wrong because it is pleasant, and avoid the right because it is painful. By habit we come to find pleasure in right action, and then the action is a true virtue as held by the Greek philosophers. Aristotle remarks: "Hence the importance of having had a certain training from very early days, as Plato says, such a training as produces pleasure and pain at the right objects; for this is the true education."

The personality of the teacher is a potent factor in moral education. Perfection is not expected of the teacher; none ever attained it except the Great Prototype. All that we can say of the best man is that he averages high. The teacher who does not possess to a somewhat marked degree some quality eminently worthy of imitation will hardly be of the highest value in his profession. I remember with gratitude two men, each of whom impressed me with a noble quality that made an important contribution at the time to my thought, feeling, action, and growth. The ideal of one was action—energetic, persevering action—and he was a notable example of his ideal. His precept without his example would have been almost valueless. The other was a noble advocate of ideal thought, and his mind was always filled with the highest conceptions; moreover, in many large ways he exemplified his precept. His acquaintance was worth more than that of a thousand others who are satisfied with a commonplace view of life.

Minds that are not speculative, are not ingenious and creative, will hardly make their own ideals, or even be taught by abstractions. They can, however, readily comprehend the living embodiment of virtue, and there is still enough of our ancestral monkey imitativeness remaining to give high value to example.

And it is important that the influence of the teacher shall not be merely a personal magnetism that influences only when it is present, but a quality that shall command respect in memory and help to establish principles of conduct. The influence should be one that will be regarded without the sanction of the personal relation. He who is wholly ruled either by fear or by love gains no power of self-control, and will be at a loss when thrown upon his own responsibility in the world of conflict and temptations. Character must be formed by habit and guided by principle.

The world's moral heroes are few. Since they can not be our daily companions, we turn to biography and history, that their personality and deeds may be painted in our imagination. Concrete teaching is adapted to children, and select tales of great and noble men, vivid descriptions of deeds worthy of emulation may early impress their minds with unfading pictures that will stand as archetypes for their future character and conduct. Hence the value of mythology, of Bible stories, and Plutarch.

It is unnecessary to add that such literature should be at the command of every teacher, and there is enough adapted to every grade of work. Throughout the period of formal historic study important use should be made of the ethical character of men and events. The pupil thus fills his mind with examples from which he may draw valuable inferences, and with which he may illustrate principles of action. The ethical sense is developed through relations of the individual to society, and the broader the scope of vision, the more just will be the estimate of human action.

Ideal literature, the better class of fiction and poetry, which not only reaches the intellect, but touches the feeling and brings the motive powers in harmony with ideal characters, deeds, and aspirations, may have the highest value in forming the ethical life of the pupil. Here is presented the very essence of the best ideas and feelings of humanity—thoughts that burn, emotions of divine quality, desires that go beyond our best realizations, acts that are heroic—all painted in vivid colors. By reading we enter into the life of greater souls, we share their aspirations, we make their treasure our own. A large share of the moralization of the world is done by this process of applying poetry to life.

There is, however, one important caution. There is a difference between sentiment and sentimentality. The latter weakens the mind and will; it is to be avoided as slow poison that will finally undermine a strong constitution. There must be a certain vigor in ideal sentiment that will not vanish in mawkish feeling, but will give tone for noble action. It is a question whether sentiment that sheds tears, and never, in consequence, does an additional praiseworthy act, has worth. You know the literature that leaves you with a feeling of stupid satiety, and you know that which gives you the feeling of strength in your limbs, and clearness in your intellect, and earnestness in your purpose, and determination in your will.

Use ideal literature from the earliest school days of the child; choose it with a wisdom that comes from a careful analysis of the subject and a knowledge of the adaptation of a particular selection to the end proposed. And when you reach the formal study of literature, find in it something more than dates, events, grammar, and rhetoric; find in it beauty, truth, goodness, and insight that will expand the mind and improve character.

There is much truth in the criticism that condemns precept without example; the two go together, the one is a complement of the other. We act in response to ideas, and a rule of action clearly understood and adopted will often be applied in a hundred specific instances that fall under it. A teacher of tact and skill can gain the interest of children to know the meaning and understand the application of many rich generalizations from human experiences that have passed into proverbs. The natural result of conduct which we condemn may be pointed out, with often a noticeable increase of regard for duty and prudence. We may not expect consistency of character, firmness of purpose, rigid observance of honesty, truthfulness, honor, and sympathy until the course of life is directed by principles that have taken firm hold of the mind.

When moral instruction in school passes into what the boys call preaching, the zealous teacher often dulls the point of any possible interest in the subject, and thereby defeats his purpose. Sometimes we, in our feeling of responsibility, trust too little to the better instincts of childhood, the influence of good surroundings, and the leavening power of all good work in the regular course of instruction.

For the purpose of moral instruction in the schools we should take the broad view of the Greek ethics. As summed up by Professor Green the Good Will aims (1) to know what is true and create what is beautiful; (2) to endure pain and fear; (3) to resist the allurements of false pleasure; (4) to take for one's self and to give to others, not what one is inclined to, but what is due. This is larger than the conventional moral code. It makes virtues not only of justice and temperance, but of courage and wisdom. By implication it condemns cowardice and lazy ignorance. It urges one to strive for the realization of all his best possibilities, to enlarge his powers, his usefulness, and aim at the gradual perfection of his being through the worthy use of all his energies. It does not dwell morbidly on petty distinctions of casuistry, but generously expands the soul to receive wisdom, the wisdom that regards all good.

We are creatures of numerous native impulses, all useful in their proper exercise. Each impulse is susceptible of growth until it becomes predominant. The lower animals follow their instincts. Man is rational, has the power to discriminate, to estimate right and wrong, to educate and be educated. He is called upon to subordinate some impulses and to cultivate others. The child is full of power of action, and it must be exercised in some direction. The work of the teacher is to invite the native impulses that reach out toward right and useful things, by offering the proper objects for their exercise. When these tendencies of the child's being are encouraged, his growth will be ethical.

What is the relation of the doctrine of duty to the practical subject in hand? This is a question that rests upon the broad foundation of philosophy and religion, and we cannot discuss the grounds of belief. We may believe that the sense of duty is indispensable to moral character. True, much has been done in the name of duty that has been harmful and repellent. Many things have been thought to be duty that would rule healthful spontaneity and cheerfulness and needful recreation out of life, and place the child under a solemn restraint that rests on his spirit like an incubus and drives him to rebellion and sin. We do not mean duty in this caricature of the reality. But this is a world in which the highest good is to be obtained by courage to overcome evil and difficulty. The great Fichte said: "I have found out now that man's will is free, and that not happiness, but worthiness is the end of our being." And Professor Royce in the same vein says: "The spiritual life isn't a gentle or an easy thing.... Spirituality consists in being heroic enough to accept the tragedy of existence, and to glory in the strength wherewith it is given to the true lords of life to conquer this tragedy, and to make their world, after all, divine." In the name of evolution and physiological psychology much good has been done in driving to the realm of darkness, whence it emanated, the spirit of harshness and cruelty in education and in discipline; at the same time much harm has been done by superficial interpreters by the attempt to make all education and training a pleasure. The highest good cannot be gained without struggle. Character cannot be formed without struggle. You and I would give nothing for acquisitions that have cost us nothing. While the child's will is to be invited in the right direction by every worthy motive that tends to make the path pleasant, the child at the same time should know by daily experience that some things must be because they are right, because they are part of his duty; that they may be at first disagreeable and require stern effort. Only then will he be prepared to resist temptation, and to actively pursue a course that will lead toward the perfection of his being and toward a life of usefulness. Along the paths of pleasure are the wrecks of innumerable lives, and this view is one of the greatest practical importance in the every-day work of the schoolroom.

All proper education is ethical education. How the teacher encourages the acquisition of truth! With what care he corrects error in experiment and inference! With what zeal he leads the pupil to further knowledge! With what feeling he points out beauty in natural forms and in literary art! With what hope he encourages him to overcome difficulties! With what solicitude he regards his ways and his choice of company! What use he makes of every opportunity to emphasize a lesson of justice in this little society of children, which is in many ways a type of the larger society into which the child is to enter! If teachers are learned and skilful, and of strong character, if they awaken interest in studies and not disgust, if they have insight into the moral order of the world as revealed in all departments of learning, the whole curriculum of study, from the kindergarten to the university, will be a disclosure of ethical conceptions, a practice of right activity, an encouragement of right aim. If the better tendencies of the child's nature are repelled instead of invited, in so far will instruction lack the ethical element. And herein lies the great responsibility of the teacher for his own education, methods, and personal influence.

What are the schools doing for moral training? We believe they are doing much that is satisfactory and encouraging. The public schools have at their command the various ethical forces. They form right habits by every-day requirements of the schoolroom; they provide the personal influence of teachers whose good character is the first passport to their position; they employ the lessons of history and literature, and in distinct ways impart principles of right conduct; they inspire courage to overcome difficulties; they direct the better impulses of children toward discovery in the great world of truth, and, by the very exercise of power required in the process of education, prepare them for life.

VII.

CAN VIRTUE BE TAUGHT?

Protagoras' view—Ethical problem of secondary schools—Analysis of impulses to action—Relation of whole school curriculum to moral development—Some specific ways of teaching practical ethics—Interest—Romanticism—Moral growth a growth in freedom.

On a certain occasion Socrates assumed the rôle of listener, while Protagoras discoursed upon the theme "Can Virtue Be Taught?" Protagoras shows that there are some essential qualities which, regardless of specific calling, should be common to all men, such as justice, temperance, and holiness—in a word, manly virtue. He holds it absurd and contrary to experience to assume that virtue cannot be taught. He says that, in fact, "Education and admonition commence in the first years of childhood, and last to the very end of life." Mother and nurse, and father and tutor ceaselessly set forth to the child what is just or unjust, honorable or dishonorable, holy or unholy; the teachers look to his manners, and later put in his hands the works of the great poets, full of moral examples and teachings; the instructor of the lyre imparts harmony and rhythm; the master of gymnastics trains the body to be minister to the virtuous mind; and when the pupil has completed his work with the instructors, the state compels him to learn the laws, and live after the pattern which they furnish. "Cease to wonder, Socrates, whether virtue can be taught."

We can but accept the principles of Protagoras, that the essential qualities of a rational and moral being are to be considered at each stage of growth and in all relations of life; that all education is to be the ally of virtue. We can but accept, too, the fact that guidance, instruction, and authority help to bring the child to self-realization, and help to determine modes of conduct. The remaining question relates to the ways and means adapted to a given stage of education. When the pupil enters the high school he is already a trained being. His training, however, has been more or less mechanical. He is now at an age when his capacity, his studies, and his social relations admit him to a broader field—a field in which he makes essays at independent action; when his physical development brings new problems and dangers; when contact with the world begins to acquaint him with the vicious maxims of selfish men; when there is a tendency to break away from the moral codes, without the wisdom of experience to guide him in his growing freedom. It is a critical period—one that tests in new ways his mental and moral balance. If the pupil is not wrecked here, he has many chances in his favor, although the college or business life or society may later sorely tempt him. That the teachings and influences of the period of secondary education have much to do with making character is recognized by the colleges. Some schools become known for the vigor of their intellectual and ethical training, and the successful preparation of their pupils to meet the demands and temptations of college life. The subject of ethics in the high school thus becomes a proper one for inquiry.

Shall we employ the formal study of ethics? Hardly. The scientific or theoretical treatment of the subject belongs to the period of reflection, of subjective insight, and should follow psychology, if not philosophy. Such study hardly accomplishes much practically until experience and reflection have given one an interest in the deepest problems of life. It belongs to a period when the commonplaces are fraught with meaning, when a rational conviction has the force which Socrates gave to insight into wisdom—when to understand virtue is to conform the life to it. But, nevertheless, the whole period of high-school work should be a contribution to the end of moral character. Let us get rid, at the outset, of the idea that a moral life is a mechanical obedience to rules and conventionalities, a cut-and-dried affair, a matter that lies in but one province of our nature, a formalism, and learn that the whole being, its purposes and activities, the heroic impulses and the commonplace duties lie within its circle. Everything a man is and does, learns and becomes, constitutes his moral character.

Ethics is the science of conduct—conduct on both its subjective and its objective side. It considers the relation of the self to all consequences of an act as foreseen and chosen by the self, and to the same consequences as outwardly expressed. Practically it teaches control of impulse with reference to results as expressing and revealing the character—results both immediate and remote. Some acts show a one-sided inclination, uncontrolled by regard for the claims of other and better impulses; only a part of the individual is asserted, not the whole self in perfect balance. For example, the pupil plays truant, acting with sole regard for the impulse to seek ease and sensuous pleasure. He neglects other more important impulses, all of which might have been satisfied by attending faithfully to his school duties: the impulse of ambition, to gain power and become a useful and successful citizen; the desire for culture, with all its superior values; the impulse of wonder, leading ever to the acquisition of knowledge; the impulse of admiration, to seek and appreciate the beautiful; the filial and social affections, which regard the feelings and wishes of the home and the sentiments of companions; the impulse to gratitude, as shown toward parents and teachers; the sentiment of reverence, as shown toward law and order and those who stand as their representatives. And all these neglected demands rise up and condemn him; he is divided from himself and his fair judgment, is not his complete self. On the other hand, the pupil spends the day in devotion to work, he maintains the integrity and balance of his nature, gives each impulse due consideration and makes a symmetrical and moral advance in his development. In restraining the impulse to play truant, he does justice to all the claims of his being; the resulting values as estimated in subjective experiences are the highest possible—the act is good. The problem, then, is to bring the pupil to a fuller understanding of the character of his impulses to action, and the relative value of each. In many ways the neglected elements of his nature may be brought into consciousness and emphasized. Everything that creates conceptions of ideal conduct, all concrete illustrations in the social life of the school, all conscious exercise of power in right ways, contribute toward his self-realization. The high-school pupil has not had a large personal experience; hence the need, in the ways proposed, of teaching virtue. In the first place, the situation is advantageous. It is conceded by every school of ethical thinkers that one finds his moral awakening in contact with society. Society is the mirror in which one sees a reflection of himself, and comes to realize himself and his character. The school of the people, which is in an important sense an epitome of that larger world which he is to enter, furnishes an admirable field for development. Moreover, it is a community where the restraint, the guidance, the ideals come of right from properly constituted authority. The whole problem of objective relations and corresponding subjective values may find illustration and experiment in the daily life of the school. The constructive imagination may be employed to infer from experiences in school to larger experiences of kindred quality in the field of life. By judging real or supposed cases of conduct the pupil makes at least a theoretical choice. By learning and interpreting characters and events in history his view is broadened.

The whole school curriculum should contribute to moral development. Whatever of intellect, emotion, and will is exercised in a rational field expands the soul normally. The pursuit of studies with the right spirit, and with regard for the activities and relations incidental thereto, is moral growth. Studies awaken rational interest, cultivate habits of industry, are devoted to the discovery of truth, reveal important relations of the individual to society, and present the purest ideals of the race. There is hardly a more valuable moralizer than healthy employment itself, employment that engages the whole man—perception, imagination, thought, emotion, and will—employment that looks toward ennobling and useful consequences, employment that has the sanction of every consideration that regards man's full development. If the studies of the high-school course do not make for good, it is because they fail to get hold of the pupil, to awaken his interest and energies. If the subject matter and the instruction are adapted to the pupil's need, if conceptions are clearly grasped, if healthy interest is aroused and the attention turns spontaneously to the work, the pupil's growth will be in every way beneficent. One who regards the moral development of his pupils will conscientiously study the method of his teaching, and learn whether the source of neglect and rebellion lies there.

The personality of the teacher is one of the most important factors in ethical training. It is ethics teaching by example; it is the living embodiment of conduct. The ideas that find expression in the life of the teacher are likely to be imitated. The sympathy of the teacher with the endeavor of the pupil infuses life into his effort. We do not refer to a certain kind of personal magnetism; this may be pernicious in the extreme. It may exist to the extent of partially hypnotizing the independent life of the pupil, robbing him for a time of part of his individuality. The ideal instructor should be earnest and noble, impressing one with the goodness, dignity, and meaning of life. An easy-going regard for duties, a half-way attachment to labor are sure to impress themselves on the minds of pupils; as readily will honor, sincerity, and pure ideals be reflected in their endeavors. You will ask: What are some of the specific ways in which a teacher may direct his efforts? We often look far for the means of accomplishment when they are already at hand. The means of moral influence are not the exclusive possession of learning or genius; they may be used by every teacher, and we should have faith in what the schools are already doing to make good character. The successful use of methods depends upon the teacher's judgment and tact. One may do harm by conscientious but ill-directed effort. With Solomon we must remember that there is a time for everything. Amongst other impulses, natural or acquired, the pupil has impulses to regard honor, honesty, truthfulness, gentlemanliness, good thoughts, respect, gratitude, sympathy, industry, usefulness. In a fit of rage, with desire to harm the object of his vindictiveness, he may disregard nearly every one of the above qualities. The impulse of anger acts blindly, heedless of external consequences and of the subjective values that attach to the execution of every desire. All cases of bad conduct, varying in degree, show a similar disproportionate estimate of the value of motives. Our problem is to plant in the consciousness of the pupil an appreciation of neglected qualities. It may be noted in passing that there are some cases of physical tendency, amounting to monomania. Conscious wrong never is able fully to conceal itself, and when the truth becomes evident to the teacher, as it may, he should seek the confidence of the home, and through the home the influence upon the pupil of a trusted physician who possesses both medical skill and moral force.

In approaching the specific ways of moral education, we may first make our obeisance to habit. The limitations as to time, place, and activity, which are incidental to all school life, help to form habits which turn the growing youth still more from the condition of uncontrolled liberty into one of well-regulated conduct, civilize him, and make him a fit member of society. Habits of regard for the rights of others further lay the foundation of altruism. Habit has its value. It establishes tendencies of conduct, although in a more or less mechanical way, which make easier the adherence to virtue in the advanced period of reflective insight. Too, these same duties mechanically performed may later be known in their full significance, and become moral acts.

The judicious use of maxims, also, has a value. Maxims are the first formal expression of the experience of the race as to the things to do or avoid. Since we act from ideas, maxims may serve practically for many concrete cases. This is especially true if the full meaning of a maxim has been presented. Next to maxims, and greater in importance, are the events and characters of history and biography. Embodied virtues and vices, real events that show the movements and reveal the motives of a people, appeal strongly to the interest. Yet, being remote in time and place, they allow the freest discussion and may be made permanent types for the instruction and improvement of mankind. The value lies in the fact that qualities thus known hasten the self-realization of the same qualities. The life of a Socrates, an Aristides, of a Cato, a Savonarola, a Luther, a Cromwell, a Lincoln, a Whittier, of all men and women who exemplify virtue, heroism, self-denial, all struggles for the right, are the high-water mark for every aspiring nature. And in the teaching of history and biography it is not necessary at every turn to deliver a homily; rather lead the pupil into the spirit and understanding of the subject—some things shine with their own light.

A yet more fertile source of ideal conceptions is the choice literature of the world. From this rich treasury we draw the poetry which we apply to life. In literature truth is given life and color, idealized and made attractive. Qualities are abstracted, refined, perfected, and glorified. They serve to show us the meaning of those qualities in us. Literature presents emotions that in their purity and refinement seem to transcend the material world; heroes and martyrs idealized and embodying self-sacrifice and devotion; sentiments that touch the whole range of chords in the heart and awaken tenderness or heroism. The pupil reads Homer and gains conceptions of heroic virtues; the "Lays of Ancient Rome," and gains ideas of perfect honor and devotion to country; Tennyson, and he follows the pure conceptions and feels that life has taken on a nobler coloring; Carlyle's doctrine of work and duty, and feels his moral sinews strengthened. Thoughts that aspire, emotions of transcendent worth, courage, heroism, benevolence, devotion to country or humanity—all these are at the command of the instructor, if he has the skill to lead the pupil into the spirit and understanding of literature. If he has not the skill, let him not touch it.

The study of science itself offers opportunities. Science searches for truth, judges not hastily, removes all prejudice, employs the judicial spirit. It should suggest lessons in fairness, justice, and truth in the field of human conduct. Hasty inference, prejudiced judgment are responsible for half the sins of this world, and the scientific spirit should be made to pass from the abstract field over into practical life.

Something can be done by daily assembly of pupils. While men have various occupations, there are certain interests that belong to men as men, as human beings. As there are hymns set to noble music which are sung for centuries without diminution of interest, because they are adapted to the want of man's essential nature, so there are gems of æsthetic and ethical literature which have stood the test of time and are approved by common consent. The reading of vigorous, healthful selections can but have an influence sooner or later upon the listener. The teacher, in a brief address, may express some thought or experience or ideal or sentiment, that will reach the inner life. In no way, however, will the good sense and skill of the teacher be put to severer test than in the selection of these teachings. They easily become monotonous instead of giving vital interest.

Professor John Dewey, in an admirable article on the subject of interest, defines it thus: "Interest is impulse functioning with reference to an idea of self-expression." He further says: "The real object of desire is not pleasure, but self-expression.... The pleasure felt is simply the reflex of the satisfaction which the self is anticipating in its own expression.... Pleasure arrives, not as the goal of an impulse, but as an accompaniment of the putting forth of activity." These expressions mean simply that the human being has native impulses to activity; that these impulses, under rational control, aim at proper ends; that pleasure is not the end of action but merely accompanies the putting forth of activity; that interest is the mental excitement that arises when the self-active mind has an end in view and the means of its attainment—a feeling that binds the attention to the end and the means. His doctrine denies hedonism. We are not to aim at a good, but to act the good. We are not to work for the pleasure, but to find pleasure in working. This is a doctrine of vast importance to the educator. External and unworthy rewards for effort are false motives. The work itself must furnish interest, because suited to the activities of the pupil. The great problem of the teacher is to invite a self-activity that finds its reward in the activity.

False motives should not be held before pupils. There is a view of life called romanticism, the condemnation of which gives Nordau his one virtue. The adherents claim for themselves the fill of a constantly varying round of completely satisfying emotional life. The history of prominent adherents of this view is a warning to this generation. The devotees either become rational and satirize their own folly, or become pessimists, railing at the whole that life has to offer, or commit suicide, and thus well rid the world of their useless presence. Carlyle points out that not all the powers of christendom combined could suffice to make even one shoeblack happy. If he had one half the universe he would set about the conquest of the other half. And then follows the grand exhortation to useful labor, the performance of duty, as the lasting source of satisfaction. If we do not find happiness therein, we may get along without happiness and, instead thereof, find blessedness. This is the doctrine of Goethe's Faust. Faust at first wishes to enjoy everything and do nothing. He runs the whole round of pleasure, of experience, and emotional life, and finds satisfaction in nothing. Finally, in the second book, he finds the supreme moment in the joy of useful labor for his fellow men. It is to be noted, however, that as soon as he is fully satisfied he dies, as, metaphorically, people in that state always do. Pleasure does not make life worth living, but living the fulness of our nature is living a life of worth.

Laying aside all theories, even the theoretical correctness of what follows, it is necessary to hold practically to the transcendental will. This is a large word, but it means simply going over beyond the mere solicitation of present pleasure, and holding with wisdom and courage to the claims of all the impulses of our being—in a word, living a life of integrity. The transcendental will can suffer and persevere and refuse pleasure, and endure and work out good and useful results. It is important to give pupils a little touch of the heroic, else they will be the sport of every wind that blows and least of all be able to withstand the tempest or the wintry blast.

There is a well-worn figure of speech, essentially Platonic in its character, which, once well in the mind of a young man or woman, will surely influence the life for good. As the healthy tree grows and expands in symmetry, beauty, and strength, and blossoms and yields useful fruit, instead of being dwarfed or growing in distorted and ugly forms, so the normal soul should expand and develop in vigor and beauty of character, and blossom and yield a life of usefulness. A stunted soul, one that has gone all awry, is a spectacle over which men and gods may weep. In some way the nobility of life, the grandeur of upright character must be impressed upon the mind of youth.

And moral growth must be growth in freedom. Rules and maxims, petty prohibitions, and restraints alone will not make morality, but rather bare mechanism and habit. Moral freedom means that, by an insight that comes of right development, one views the full bearing of any problem of conduct, and chooses with a wisdom that is his own. Morality is not mechanism, but insight. Doctrine does not constitute morality. Pharisaism is immorality and will drive any one to rebellion and sin. Mechanical rule has no vitalizing power. A moral life should be self-active, vigorous, joyous, and free. So far as spontaneous conduct can be made to take the place of rule and restraint will you secure a growth that will expand, when, well-rooted by your fostering care, you finally leave it to struggle with the elements.

Following in substance the thought of a prominent educator,—not so much pedagogical preaching as skilful stimulating, not so much perfect ideals as present activities, not so much compulsion as inviting self-activity are to-day the needs of the schools. Through guidance of present interest the child may later attain to the greater interests of life in their full comprehension.

VIII.

COLLEGE AND UNIVERSITY.[2]

Summary of answers to inquiries—The college and preparation—Liberal education—The college and active life—Ethical ideals—University standards.

Touching the theme of higher education, inquiries were sent to a large number of universities, colleges, and secondary schools. The first two questions related to the work of secondary education, and were as follows: (1) What should the high-school graduate be when entering college? (2) What does he lack of an ideal education when he enters? Considering the general character of the questions, the answers were all that might be expected, and they are valuable for the limit of their range, as well as for what they express, since they show that, concerning the main purpose of education, there is nothing new to be said.

The following are opinions that represent the majority or appear important as individual views: (1) The high-school graduate, when entering college, should possess a mind educated by methods that create interest and make power to think and generalize—power to do original work. (2) He should have an acquaintance with each field of knowledge, and should show a symmetrical development of his mental activities. (3) As tending to produce greater interest, knowledge, and power, he should have been trained in only a limited number of subjects in each field; in these subjects the work should have been continuous and intensive. (4) He should have good command of English. (5) He should be well-grounded in right habits and moral principles—the practice of self-control.

While this inquiry is not strictly upon the subject, it shows that the difficult problems of university life are to be solved in part by the secondary schools, and that some of the failures in higher education are due to the imperfections of earlier training. It also introduces part of the discussion that follows.

The third question pertained to higher education: What should the college or university do for the high-school graduate? Some of the more important opinions received may be expressed as follows:

(a) It should supplement the failures of his earlier training. There should be no chasm between secondary and higher education.

(b) It should give him a liberal education; it should offer him a course that has

[2] Read before the National Association of City Superintendents, at Jacksonville, Florida, in 1896.

unity and harmony. It should cultivate the power of research. It should teach him to bring all his knowledge and all his power to bear on the problems of life.

(c) It should make him broad, and then deep in some subject. It should start him in lines of study leading to his life work.

(d) It should give him high ideals of private and civic conduct; it should make a man of him.

To consider merely the subject of college ideals would be trite and unprofitable, and some latitude will be used in the discussion.

The influence of the college should be felt in the work of preparation. That the college should be closely articulated with the high schools is an idea of modern date, but one that now is received with growing favor. An examination of the admission requirements of the colleges still shows a variety of demands, having no common basis in principles of education, in the standard courses of high schools, or in uniform agreement. The requirements of some colleges are imperative for specific subjects that are not fundamental, but merely rank with a series of allied subjects in a given field of knowledge. Often a method of work acceptable to one college would be rejected by another. Among reputable institutions the height of the standard varies by two years.

The dissatisfaction of the high schools with these evils is deep-seated and wide-spread. The fault rests mainly with the colleges and universities, and the reasons that maintain unessential distinctions are absurd in the eyes of secondary-school men. If absolute uniformity in college admission is not feasible, a reasonable choice of equivalents within a given department of knowledge may be allowed. At least a plan of admission may be *"organized without uniformity."* A college has been known to refuse four years' excellent work in science as a substitute for some chapters in a particular book on physical geography. In another instance a certain scientific school, requiring two years of preparation in Latin, refused a four years' course in Latin in lieu of the prescribed number of books in Cæsar. A joint committee has recently been appointed by the Department of Higher Education and the Department of Secondary Education, of the National Educational Association, to consider further the basis of connection between the high schools and the colleges. This committee consists of eminent and able men, who will accomplish important results, if given proper encouragement and aid by the National Association, and if the various local associations coöperate, instead of fostering organized differences.[3] The report of the Committee of Ten did much to prepare

[3] This committee made its report in 1899. The committee recommend that any study, included in a given list regarded as suitable for the secondary-school period, and pursued under approved conditions one year of four periods a week, be regarded as worthy to count toward admission to college; they recognize that not all secondary schools are equipped to offer all the subjects, and that the colleges will make their own selections for admission; they recognize the principle of large liberty to the student in secondary schools, but do not believe in unlimited election, and they emphasize the importance of certain constants in all secondary schools and in all requirements for admission to college; they recommend that these constants be recognized in the following proportion: Four units in foreign languages

the way for a more complete and satisfactory connection between the colleges and the high schools, but much remains to be done which may well be undertaken by this joint committee. It is interesting to note that one of the longest sections in the report of the Royal Commission on Secondary Education is on the "Relation of the University to Secondary Education," and that the importance of a close connection is emphasized and the means of securing it is suggested.

The work of secondary education must be based on pedagogical principles and adapted to the stage of development which it represents, and the colleges must take up the work where the high schools leave it. Whatever is best for a given period of growth is also good preparation for what follows. There should be no *saltus* in the process of general education. We do not mean that the colleges are not to help determine the preparatory courses of study; but they must regard the natural order of development in grades below the college as well as ideal college standards.

By a closer union with the high schools, the colleges may help to fashion their courses, improve their methods, and may suggest the importance of placing college-educated men and women in charge of the various departments of high-school work. The report of the Royal Commission previously referred to, discussing the preparation of teachers for the secondary schools, says: "So far as regards general education, they will obtain it, and, in our opinion, ought to obtain it, not in special seminaries, but in the same schools and universities as are resorted to by persons desiring to enter the other professions. The more attractive the profession becomes, the larger will be the number of teachers who will feel that they ought to fit themselves for it by a university course." The report further says: "Whatever professional education is provided for teachers ought to have both a theoretical and a practical side.... Freedom and variety would, in our opinion, be best secured, if the universities were to take up the task; ... and, if the science of education is to make good the claims put forward in its behalf, it ought to be studied where other branches of mental and moral philosophy are fully handled by the ablest professors."

Many colleges are doing much to increase laboratory practice in the high schools, to cultivate the spirit of investigation, to limit the number of subjects and secure good results. In one of the new States, Colorado, the principle is generally (no language accepted in less than two units), two units in mathematics, two in English, one in history, and one in science.

The thirteenth annual convention (1900) of the Association of Colleges and Preparatory Schools of the Middle States and Maryland passed resolutions urging the establishment of a joint college-admission examination board to bring about an agreement upon a uniform statement as to each subject required by two or more colleges for admission, to hold examinations, and to issue certificates to be accepted by the Middle-State Colleges.

At the Charleston meeting of the N. E. A. (1900) the following resolution was passed: "*Resolved,* That the Department of Secondary Education and the Department of Higher Education of the National Educational Association commend the Report of the Special Committee on College-Entrance Requirements, as affording a basis for the practical solution of the problem of college admission, and recommend the Report to the attention of the colleges of the country."

recognized that a good preparatory education is also a good general education, and that every high school is, therefore, a preparatory school. The secondary-school period is maintained at four years, laboratories are provided in all the schools, and Latin and German, if not Greek, are found in all. These results are largely due to the close relation in that State between secondary and higher education.

In the second group of opinions quoted, the philosophy is Platonic rather than materialistic or utilitarian. It makes a student a man of ideal powers, possibilities, and aspirations. He possesses a nature whose development is an end in itself, whose well-being is of prime consideration. Liberal education aims to give the student a conscious realization of his powers, without reference to material advantage through their use in a given occupation or profession. Through liberal education the student acquires ideas of universal interest and essential character. He gains a comprehensive view that enables him to estimate things at their relative value, to learn the place, use, and end of each.

That liberal education should remain the ideal of at least a large part of the college course, most educators agree. Were this function of the college not a distinctive and essential one, that department of learning would of necessity be abandoned, and the direct road to practical business would be pursued. Recent addresses, representing three of the greatest American universities, agree that the function of the college is to be maintained, and that acquaintance with the several fields of knowledge is necessary to the very idea of liberal education. They agree to include the field of the languages and literature, the field of the sciences and mathematics, the subjective field, that of philosophy and psychology. In a late report of the Commissioner of Education appears a German criticism of American education, which mentions the lack of linguistic training. The writer says: "The consequences are seen in the defective linguistic-logical discipline of the mind, which perhaps more than the discipline in the mathematical forms of thought is a requisite of all profound intellectual progress, be that in linguistic or in mathematical and scientific branches." In the University of Berlin, philosophy is a required subject for all degrees.

The conservation of the ideals of the race is largely the work of liberally educated men. Some one has argued that not through education, but through a higher standard of society and politics, will the youth of the land be reached; but society and politics depend upon ideal education and the church for their own purification.

The power of research is characteristic of modern university training and is essential to a liberal education, as giving one the mastery of his powers. Carlyle was not far from the right when he said that the true university is a library. The ability to use a library is one criterion of successful college work. Here the student gathers his own material, uses his own discrimination, formulates his opinions in the light of numerous facts and opinions, and gains self-reliance. It is the scientific method, as taught by Socrates, applied to all fields of study. This is the kind of work that prepares the student to grapple with the practical problems of the day.

The opinion that some portion of the college work should be prescribed appears to be well founded. This view is strengthened by the fact that many high schools are weak in one or more departments of preparation. A minimum of required work in leading departments of the college will tend to supply the deficiencies of previous training. From an inspection of the latest college catalogues it appears that all colleges exercise some kind of supervision over the choice of studies, and many of them prescribe and determine the order of more than half the curriculum. In choice of electives many require the group system, in order that consistency may be maintained and that a definite result in some line of work may be reached.

The line of demarcation between college and university work is a variable, and the problem of definitely locating it is perplexing in the extreme. Many believe they see signs of segmentation at the end of the junior year and predict that the senior year will adhere to the graduate school. There are many evidences that somewhere along the line the period of general education will be shortened, and the tendency to specialize before the end of the college course is one proof that the change is demanded. Historically the college in America stands as a whole for liberal education, but in its later development the standard has been advanced and the period of professional education has been lengthened until the problem presents new phases demanding important readjustments. Replies recently received from many institutions of higher learning, touching this question, show a variety of opinions. One correspondent pithily says, "Verily, we are a smattering folk. I believe both the college and the professional course should be lengthened." President Eliot advocates "a three years' course for the A.B., without disguises or complications." Estimating the replies already received numerically, something more than half favor some kind of time readjustment, to the end that the period covered by the college and the professional school may be shortened one year.

While defending liberal education, it may be held that, especially while a four years' college course is maintained, it should also look toward the world of active influence, and the filling of some vocation therein. The student's duties toward society must take on the modern aspect, as contrasted with the self-centred interest of the mediæval recluse. That education should aim at mere serene enjoyment of the True, the Beautiful, and the Good is an idea of the past. The mere recluse today has no meaning and no use in the world. Educated men must join the march of progress; they must take part in the solution of ethical problems, in the bettering of government and society. The world demands of them altruism, public spirit, high ideals. They should mass the forces of the past for an onward movement in the present. Old knowledge should reach out toward new and useful applications.

To these ends the college should provide for a deeper knowledge of some subject or group of related subjects. This is an essential element of general education, and also has a practical aim. The principles of the philosophical and social sciences should find concrete illustration in the present. And above all, student life should be inspired with ideas of the duties and responsibilities of citizenship.

A public statement has been made that the seniors of a well-known university have less intellectual vigor and less moral power than the average man they might meet on the streets. If the charge be true, it is a matter for serious thought, but the statement should be swallowed with a large grain of salt. It may, however, serve as a text. The college must assume an amount of responsibility for the character of the undergraduate student. There has been a natural reaction against some of the unwise requirements of twenty-five years ago, but the reaction may have gone too far. One of our famous universities ten years ago adopted the policy of leaving the student to his own devices and the moral restraint of the policeman, but the plan was condemned by the patrons of the institution, and to-day it exercises a wise and friendly care over the student's choice of studies, his attendance upon lectures, and his daily walk and conversation. Entire freedom in student life belongs only to the graduate schools, and to place both undergraduate and graduate students under one system can but prove harmful.

The ethical problems of college life are not to be solved wholly by perfunctory religious exercises, but by the spirit that pervades the whole teaching and student body, and by the many ways and means that the united efforts of earnest and devoted faculties may employ. It is a favorable circumstance that the student to an extent can choose subjects in accord with his tastes; that his powers may reach out toward some great intellectual interest. That the spirit of education is broader, more liberal, and scientific is significant; the fact makes for truth and honesty. The historical method succeeds the dogmatic in history, social science, philosophy, and ethics. Men are better because they are broader and wiser and are coming to a higher realization of truth.

No doubt the ethical life has the deepest significance for man. The great Fichte was right in claiming that, if this is merely a subjectively phenomenal world, it is a necessary creation of mind that we may have it wherein to work and ethically develop. That institution will turn out the best men where the Baconian philosophy is combined with the Platonic, the scientific with the ideal. By some means the student should constantly come in contact with strong manhood and high ideals. It makes a practical difference whether the student believes in his transcendent nature and possibilities or in mere materialism and utilitarianism, whether his ethics is ideal or hedonistic, his view of life optimistic or pessimistic.

If the question is made distinct, What should the university do for the student?—there are some additional considerations.

It is enough to say of graduate courses that they should be a warrant for extended and thorough knowledge of a group of related subjects, and for original power to grasp and deal with difficult problems. The candidate's knowledge and power should be publicly tested by a good old-fashioned examination and defence of thesis.

The university should refuse to admit the student to the professional schools until he has received at least the equivalent of a complete high-school education. The faculties of the University of Colorado have made an investigation of the standard of admission to the professional schools, the length of professional courses, and the relation of the professional courses to the college. The results are of interest.[4] Very few schools of applied science in the universities require four years of preparation. Only three or four universities require that standard for their law or medical schools. Most catalogues read after this fashion: Admission to law or medical school—a college diploma, or a high-school diploma, or a second-grade teacher's certificate, or evidence of fitness to pursue the subject. Less than half of the law schools require entrance qualifications, and only twenty of them require a three years' course. All medical schools advocate a thorough scientific foundation, many of them in a very ideal way, and urge extensive laboratory practice in many special subjects. The most of them think the first two years of a medical course could well be spent without clinical work. Many colleges and collegiate departments of universities provide electives that are accepted by some schools of theology, law, or medicine for their regular first-year work. In rare instances, studies covering two years are made common to the college and the professional schools. But only a few universities have within their own organization a plan for shortening the period of college and professional study.

The "Report on Legal Education," 1893, issued by the United States Bureau of Education, says: "Admission to the bar in all Continental (European) countries is obtained through the universities which are professional schools for the four learned professions—theology, medicine, law, and philosophy. In England and America the colleges and universities are chiefly schools for general culture; only a few offer provision for thorough professional studies. While in England and America the erroneous idea is still predominant that a collegiate education need not necessarily precede professional study, in Continental Europe it is made a *conditio sine qua non*. No one more needs than the lawyer the power of general education to grasp all the facts relating to a subject, to weigh their value, discard the unessential, and give prominence to the determining factors; no one more needs the power to avoid fallacies and to argue intelligently scientific points which may be involved in litigation. No one more than the physician needs an acquaintance with psychology and philosophy, with the various sciences and the modern languages; no one more needs the power of judgment in view of seemingly contradictory facts and symptoms; no one more needs the ethical quality of the noble and honorable gentleman. Let the American universities maintain the standards which in theory they all are ready to advocate."

---

[4] During the four years (1896-1900) since this investigation was made, there has been great progress throughout the country. The standard universities now require at least a high-school education for admission to professional schools, and offer four years in medicine and three years in law.

IX.

UNIVERSITY IDEALS.[5]

Historical—The State University—Some university problems.

To an extent a university must represent the philosophy of a people at a given epoch, and their political, social, and industrial tendencies. It symbolizes the stage of civilization and spiritual insight. The ethical need of the time led to the study of philosophy in Greece; the innate regard of the Roman people for justice and the problems attending the development of the Empire emphasized the study of law in Rome; Christianity and the influence of the Greek philosophy made theology the ideal of the Middle Ages; the development of the inductive method places emphasis on physical science to-day; the industrial spirit of America gives a practical turn to our higher education. It is no mere accident that the English university is conservative and aristocratic and aims at general culture, that the French faculties are practical, or that the German universities are scientific and democratic. The differences in spirit and method are determined by factors that belong to the history and character of the different peoples.

The colleges of New England were founded on the traditions of Oxford and Cambridge, and embodied their ideal and theological aims and conservative method, although they naturally were more liberal and democratic than the parent institutions. The history of the early American colleges has been varied, but the more successful ones have certainly become catholic and progressive. As the country grew and men pushed westward, leaving tradition behind and developing more freely the spirit of our advancing civilization, the conception of a university, in touch with all the people, and scientific and free, arose. Thus we have the state university. At the same time the leading religious denominations have vied with each other in founding in the new states colleges or universities that are more or less denominational in spirit and aim.

The American university of to-day contains many elements. Broadly speaking, it represents the ideals of the Platonic philosophy, the direct inheritance from England, the character of the German university, the modern scientific method, and the practical demands of American civilization. All these elements are woven into the web of our national life. There is, of course, much diversity. Each class of

---

[5] Read at the National Council of Education, Milwaukee, July 6, 1897. This is one of three papers on "University Ideals" there presented, the other two representing respectively Princeton and Leland Stanford, Jr. The author was requested to write on "State University Ideals."

universities contains something of all the ideals, but each emphasizes certain ones. The older and larger denominational school is more nearly the direct representative of English education, but has made a great advance. The state universities represent the people as such and the tendencies of our civilization, but in accord with the highest ideals. They more readily accept the influence of the German university. The denominational colleges scattered throughout the West aim to perpetuate the denominational idea.

Almost from the foundation of our Government free elementary schools have been regarded as an essential and characteristic part of our American institutions. They became a logical necessity when our forefathers abjured the caste and intolerance of the Old World, and with prophetic insight proclaimed the era of a new civilization in which the welfare of the state should mean the welfare of all the people. While the idea of education at the expense of the state, and under its control, was early accepted in that part of the country which has gradually influenced the whole nation, we of to-day have witnessed a part of the struggle to place on a permanent foundation the modern system of high schools. These schools, especially in the West, now have an assured position and command the confidence of the people. The attempt to take the next step and establish state universities was met with doubt and opposition. At a comparatively recent date, however, many state universities have come into prominence, and to-day they appear in the main to be the coming institutions of university training from Ohio to Oregon, and from Texas to Montana. Here is a development that is remarkable, and we may well examine its significance.

In the first place the state university is the logical outcome of our democratic ideal that made the public schools a necessity, an outcome which naturally would be first realized in the newer states. As America furnished new and favorable conditions for the development of civilization, freed in part from the traditions of the Old World, so the new states of the West became the field for a still more liberal growth of the tendencies of the age. There is a recognized tendency in our institutions toward a broader community of interests in respect to many things that affect the common welfare, and in no way does this tendency find a grander expression than in the means for elevating the people at the expense of the people to a better citizenship, higher usefulness, and wiser and nobler manhood. The safety of the state depends upon giving the brightest and best of all classes and conditions an opportunity to rise to the surface of affairs.

In Prussia, Switzerland, and Italy a healthy organization of society is held to depend upon public control of both secondary and higher education. England's system of education tends to maintain social distinctions and an intellectual conservatism that are harmful both to the aristocracy and to the common people. Education in Germany shows its superiority in that it reaches a larger number of the poor classes and develops greater freedom of thought. The public control of education makes it democratic and progressive, and strengthens its influence with the people. It makes the scholar a leader in the line of advance indicated by the ideals of the people. In the American state university, men come together as a faculty, bringing with them training and educational ideals gained in the best universities of the world. They place themselves in touch with the public schools, the press, and all the state agencies of influence and control. Knowing the needs and demands of the people, they take the lead in the line of natural progress. The state university is inseparably linked to the state, and must carry with it the best influences of the state, and thus extend its influence to the whole people.

The great denominational schools at first represented homogeneous elements in the national life. Harvard was essentially a state institution. It was founded in "accord with the fundamental principles of the Commonwealth of Massachusetts." The people of Massachusetts, at that time, were largely homogeneous in race, religion, and love of freedom. Yale was founded partly on the conservative Congregationalism of Connecticut; hence it represented the mass of people in that State. Princeton was founded in the interest of the Scotch and Scotch-Irish political and religious views in the Middle States, but was so far catholic as to enlist the sympathy of the Dutch and the Quakers. However, it served a comparatively homogeneous people. In later years each of these universities, in order to reach large numbers of people maintaining diverse views, has been obliged to subordinate specific sectarian or denominational elements and emphasize only the highest ideals common to its constituency. The newer states of the West have a mixed population with heterogeneous interests. Hence it follows that not a denominational school, but a state school, broad enough for all the people, alone can satisfy the need of each state. Since it is impossible to maintain a real university for each peculiar interest, all must unite to support one institution, an institution maintaining the highest ideals common to humanity, and specifically to our own civilization. The ideals common to the American people are ample enough for an ideal university, founded and maintained by the state. Harvard or Princeton may say: "We have done for the state all that the state university claims as its function." Then let each state have a Princeton which from the start is assured of an adequate foundation. In our Western states the same reason that would create one denominational college would create in each state fifteen or twenty. The history of the world never has seen such a dissipation of educational energy as is now seen in America, and a system of state education which tends to correct the evil merits enthusiastic support. It may be added that the state university exists in the West because the majority of the people are coming to prefer that kind of institution.

We may say, then, that the state university represents (1) the completion of the democratic ideal of public education; (2) the unity of progress amidst diversity of view, and the mutual influence of the knowledge and power of the scholar and the ideals of the people; (3) the broad platform upon which the heterogeneous elements of the state may unite in the interest of higher education. It is understood, of course, that these three statements are not altogether mutually exclusive.

These views of the *raison d'être* of the state university lead directly to the presentation in detail of some facts in its history and some of its aims, showing that its ideals are practicable.

The state university virtually, if not formally, is a part of the public-school system. As such it holds a peculiar and influential relation toward the public high schools. It furnishes teachers trained in the university in regular and pedagogical courses. It scrutinizes the courses of study and the character of the work, and formally approves the schools of standard merit. It helps in every prudent way the influence of the school with the community. By its friendly relation it may present freely the advantages of higher education and thus reach a large number who would otherwise rest at the goal of high-school graduation. In every state, through the agency of the university, the number of high schools is materially increased, and their standards, plan of organization, and methods are improved. Moreover, it gives the promise of something beyond that stimulates the efforts of pupils in every grade of work.

The connection between the high school and the university still gives rise to troublesome problems, not alone in this country. The ideals of the older American university are often at variance with the systematic development of education below the university and the demands of the people. The state university has come nearer than any other to the solution. While Harvard and Yale met the growing demands of science by establishing separate schools, Michigan introduced the scientific course into the college, making it rank with the classical. This plan, generally adopted by the state universities, places them nearly in line with the natural development of the public-school system. The state universities also show their regard for popular demand by admitting special students.

By offering free tuition, the state university reaches many who would otherwise fail to enjoy higher training. It tends to equalize the conditions for rich and poor in the struggle for the survival of the fittest.

The state university, as it develops and realizes its true function, must be thoroughly catholic in spirit, because it stands for humanity, truth, and progress. Nowhere is the professor or the scholar permitted to use such intellectual freedom as in the state university in Germany, and in the natural course of events the same freedom will be allowed in the United States. Not only will the free and inventive spirit become characteristic, but our Western universities, standing in the midst of the most advanced ideas of civilization, must furnish some of the most important contributions to the study of all social, economic, and ethical problems.

In the state universities the mental and moral atmosphere is healthful. A strong, honest manhood is cultivated. There all ideals are strongly maintained, not according to a particular creed, but with regard to all the implications of man's higher nature. All influences tend to make citizens who are in harmony with the national spirit. An extended acquaintance with graduates of various state universities shows that, as a whole, they are broad-minded citizens, loyal to the public interest.

The relation of the religious denominations to the state university is one that commands serious attention. The university says to each class of people: "Here is an institution which is equally for the advantage of all—it is yours. Its platform, founded on ideals of truth, beauty, and goodness, is as broad as humanity. Since there must be diversity of religious views, establish your theological schools, halls, guilds, or professorships in the vicinity of the university, and, making use of what the state offers, supplement in your own way the work of the state." The plan is in the highest degree economical; it combines unity of effort with variety of independent view; it makes the general good and the special interest mutually helpful. It is the plan of business common sense and of wise insight into the problems of the age. That the denominations—granting their point of view—should join their interest with that of the state university is shown also by the fact that often a given denomination finds more of its students there than at its church school.

Many state universities are beginning to receive private endowment. Every consideration of public interest in each state should turn the contributions for education toward the one great centre of learning. Very few states can support more than one such centre. Libraries, art collections, museums, laboratories, buildings, well-endowed chairs, beautiful grounds, should testify to the munificence of private wealth as well as to the benefactions of the state.

Speaking generally, the state universities have large incomes and good facilities. They require high standards for admission and graduation. Wherever feasible, they maintain professional schools and schools of applied science. They do this upon the theory that the state should both regulate and provide professional education in the interest of proper standards, and that, in the interest of the state and of the individual, such education should be made available to the sons of the poor. Every leading state university is developing a graduate school.

In the matter of electives, the state university occupies a middle ground. Yale and Princeton represent the conservative side, and Harvard and Stanford the liberal extreme. An examination of the curricula of ten leading state universities shows that the requirements for admission are definitely prescribed, although two or more courses are recognized; that about half the college studies are required, while the remaining half are offered as group or free electives. The state universities naturally show a tendency toward the German university system.

In America the college has been frankly maintained in accord with Platonic ideals. A full rounded manhood, drawing its power from each chief source of knowledge, and prepared in a general way for every practical activity, has been the aim. The American college is dear to the people, and it has done much to make strong men who have powerfully influenced the nation. There are, however, various tendencies which are likely to modify the whole organization of the American university, including that of the college.

The recent tendency toward free election, reaching even into the high school, is a subject of animated controversy. This tendency I have frequently discussed elsewhere, and must still maintain that, in its extreme form, it is irrational. One university of high standing makes it possible to enter its academic department and graduate without mathematics, science, or classics. This is an extreme that is not likely to be sanctioned by the educational world. If there is a human type with characteristics by which it is defined—characteristics which can be developed only by looking toward each field of knowledge—then a secondary and higher education which makes possible the entire omission of any important group of subjects is likely to prove a great wrong to the average student. According to some high educational authorities, no one can be called liberally educated who does not at least possess knowledge of (1) mathematics and science, (2) language and literature, (3) philosophy. Philosophy, as it was in Greece and as it is in Germany, may become a larger factor in our American education.

There is another tendency which is working toward an inevitable result. The average American student who desires higher or professional education will not spend four years in high school, four years in college, and three or four years in a graduate or professional school. There is a movement to shorten in some manner the whole course of education. Already many colleges and collegiate departments of universities offer electives that will count for one or two years of law, medicine, or theology. Already the *university system* in the form of group electives is introduced into the last two years of college.

The outcome will probably be a gradual reorganization of the high-school studies and those of the first two or three years of college. The new curriculum should lay for the student a broad and firm foundation in knowledge and power for all subsequent aptitudes. Upon this should be built the graduate school, the professional school, and perhaps the school of technology. In this plan the American college need not be lost, for the bachelor's degree could be granted for a given amount of work beyond the college in the graduate school. The claim that the student should begin university work almost anywhere along the line of education, before laying a complete foundation for a specialty, appears absurd. It may be added that only by partial reorganization of our educational system can the admission standard to the American professional school ever be made respectable.

The scientific spirit—the term is used in the broadest sense—in all investigation and instruction is a most encouraging feature of present tendencies. If the American professor cannot always be an original investigator, he may keep abreast of investigation and impart its inspiration to the student. To this end the *Lehrfreiheit*, freedom in teaching, is necessary. It is a sad comment that the spirit of the inquisition has recently appeared in a New England university. The professor's thought must not be prescribed for him by any creed, religious, political, or scientific. Of course, he must stand on the safe foundation of the past—he is not expected to soar in a balloon or leap over a precipice. A recent work on "The Ideal of Universities" says: "We can distinguish four chief currents in the theology of the present era: (1) The Roman Catholic; (2) the Protestant; (3) that objective-historic theology which simply states the origin and development of the Christian doctrine; and (4) the inception of a theology based upon recognized facts of science, of human nature, and of history." All philosophy of nature and of human nature must become truth-seeking—this is a mere truism. No philosophy or belief can afford to maintain any other attitude. Leaders in the orthodox churches are teaching us this fact by their bearing toward new conceptions. And we need have no fear of the outcome. The highest ideals and hopes of humanity will be confirmed by the most thorough investigation in which metaphysics shall use the contribution of every department of objective and subjective science. A course in theology, scientific theology, should be found in every university, including the state university—and some dare to think the latter is the place for it. The facts of man's higher intellectual and emotional life are the most important data for investigation.

The doctrine of *Lernfreiheit,* the freedom of the student, unhappily has been ignorantly applied in this country. It may properly be employed for the German university student at the age of twenty to twenty-five, after his training in the gymnasium, but not to the American college student at the age of eighteen to twenty-two. In America it may apply to the students in the graduate school. Some American colleges have tried the extreme theory of mental and moral freedom for the college student, and have learned from an unsatisfactory experience the lesson of a wise conservatism.

The old struggle between science and the humanities still goes on. We must adopt a view of education which regards the nature of man and its adaptation to the whole environment, including its historical element. In a keen analysis of the *nature of things* we shall not find Greek and Latin, but we shall find them historically in our language and literature, and in the generic concepts of our civilization. Hence they are a necessary part of any extended study of language, literature, or art.

We do not believe that the practical tendency of American education will destroy our reverence for what the Germans call the *philosophical faculty* in the university. The liberal arts, including pure science, are the gems of human culture, and are given a high value even in the imagination of the ignorant. The editor of "The Cosmopolitan" draws a bold and somewhat original outline for modern education, and it is in many ways suggestive. But the author overlooks what every true scholar knows, that thorough scientific knowledge of principles must remain the fundamental work of education and the substantial ground of progress in civilization. A university course may not consist chiefly of lectures upon prudential maxims, such as all must learn partly from experience. Such a theory would award the palm, not to Socrates, but to the Sophists. The truth in all the clamor for practical work in the college is that the culture studies must be vivified by closer relation to the real world and to modern life.

Little has been said of what is called the graduate school. Germany credits us with eleven institutions that have either reached the standard of a genuine university or are rapidly approaching it. Of these eleven, five are state universities. This estimate, of course, is made in accord with the plan and standard of the German university. It appears certain that in time the name university in America will be applied only to those institutions which maintain the graduate school and raise the dignity of the professional schools. The university system will develop freely in this country only after a somewhat important reorganization of our higher education. The line must be drawn more sharply between foundation education and university work, the whole period of education must be somewhat shortened, and, in most of our universities, the graduate faculty must be strengthened. That these changes will be wrought, and that we shall have a rapid development of the genuine university is certain. Much is to be expected from our higher scholarship in many lines of investigation. In America, men are solving problems the existence of which has only been dimly conceived by the masses of people in the Old World.

Inspired by our advanced conceptions of government and society, and by the free, inventive, truth-seeking spirit characteristic of our people, the American scholar will make leading contributions to the world's literature of sociology, politics, and science. And when the spirit of reality, now superficial, gains a deeper insight into the nature of things, America may yet lead the world in those investigations which belong to the sphere of philosophy.

X.

GENERAL EDUCATION PRACTICAL.

Practical bearing of all education—World still demands liberal education, Æsthetic and ideal elements.

The possibilities of education depend upon inborn capacities, but the unfolding of them is education. A man of large capacity, born among savages, remains a savage, an Arab is a Mohammedan, an Englishman is a Christian, a child among thieves is a thief, a child in a home of culture imbibes refinement and truth. Tennyson, in the interior of Africa, would not have developed his exquisite rhyme and rhythm, metaphor and verse, and polish and sparkle of expression, would not have conceived thoughts that penetrate the earth and the nature of man, and shoot upward to the quivering stars; he would have mused under his palm tree, and have fed, perhaps somewhat daintily, upon unlucky missionaries. An African of natural ability in the homes of Massachusetts, under the influence of Harvard, would become a man of vigorous thought and fine feeling, possibly of genius.

Since education is so potent, what shall the nature of it be? Shall knowledge of mountain and forest and the seasons, and the common sense that grows from experience, and the practical power to read and compute be sufficient? If all minds were equal, if the stores of wisdom were valueless, if special investigators found nothing worth revealing, if thoughts of master minds did not inspire, if men, like brutes, were governed by instincts and had no possibilities beyond a certain physical skill, the education of nature might suffice.

This is a practical age, and no picture too bright can be drawn of the advantages of a high material civilization for bettering the condition of all classes of men. The necessity of being an active factor in the world of usefulness cannot be too strongly urged. But our material progress is dependent upon soul activity. This activity is nourished by general education. Soul activity finds expression in a thousand practical ways. We educate highly that the man may have more power, that he may have many resources, that he may do better what he has to do, and may not be dependent on one means of support or one set of conditions. It is not so much labor with the hands as intelligent directive power which is needed, and this power is largely derived from general education. Intelligent men are intelligent laborers. An educated man will learn more quickly, work more successfully, and attain a higher standard than the ignorant artisan. Theory teaches and practice proves that in business and manual pursuits educated men bring an intelligence to their work and accomplish results impossible for the ignorant man; that, as a class, they average high in all practical activities. There should be no haste to enter a trade. Life is long enough to accomplish all that may be done, and all the preparation made for its duties is a wise economy. It is hardly necessary here to state the inference that general education is practical education.

The demand for less of general education before the special is prominent. This demand does not necessarily imply that its authors believe there is too much preparation for life work; indeed, few of them would wish that preparation to be less; they would simply change the ratio between general and special training. We believe that a critical examination of rational courses of study in the schools would show that little of the work could well be omitted; that nearly all contributes toward the end of a well-rounded education, indeed is necessary to that end; and that the training of faculty is only well begun at the end of the high-school course. Even the study of the classics, besides other incidental advantages, trains the critical powers, refines the taste, and is in an important sense a subjective study. The inference is that, with less of general education, the forces of one's being would not be properly trained and marshalled for active service in life.

If we define practical education as that which is capable of being turned to use or account, a high degree of general education before the special is eminently practical, inasmuch as it broadens and heightens a man's possibilities. Moreover, it is of service to all that even a few should be educated ideally. Such education places ideals before men which tend to elevate them. We cannot easily estimate the value to the world of a genius, one of those men who stand on nature's heights and see with clear vision, and proclaim the glories of their view to listening men, who picture at least feebly the things described. They are the heralds of new events, the inspirers of progress. A highly educated man, though not a genius, in a way may occupy a similar place, and may repay by his influence, many times, in practical ways, the expense of his education. Societies of laborers are already beginning to ascribe their troubles in part to lack of education, and are looking to education as a means of improving their condition. General education is practical education.

While every boy should be taught to earn a living, this should not be done needlessly at the expense of the higher development of the faculties. Too much attention to the practical dwarfs the powers, limits the horizon, and will result in the destruction of that spirit which makes a strong national character. There is little need to urge the practical; the more immediate and obvious motives constantly draw men toward it. The refinements of the soul are at first less inviting; they are hard to gain and easy to lose. Carlyle says: "By our skill in Mechanism, it has come to pass that, in the management of external things, we excel all other ages, while in whatever respects the pure moral nature, in true dignity of soul and character, we are, perhaps, inferior to most civilized ages.... The infinite, absolute character of Virtue has passed into a finite, conditioned one; it is no longer a worship of the Beautiful and Good, but a calculation of the profitable.... Our true deity is Mechanism. It has subdued external nature for us, and we think it will do all other things." Carlyle possessed a true insight when he penned these words. Popular demands tend to make the age more unpoetic than it is. In this age the tourney has been converted into a fair; the vision of the poet is obscured by the smoke of factories; Apollo no longer leads the Immortal Nine upon Parnassus; and we would dethrone the gods from Olympus.

Men and peoples have made permanent contributions to the world's progress, not by military achievement or accumulation of wealth, but by the something better called culture. The glory of the Greeks lay not in their civil wars, but in the spirit brought to the defence of their country at Thermopylæ; not in the cost and use of their temples and statuary, but in the art that found expression in them; not in their commerce, but in the lofty views of their philosophers and the skill of their poets. Men admire that which ennobles, without thought of price or utility, and the world still demands liberal education. Literature and philosophy have much more in them for the average student than has yet been gained from them. The æsthetic side of literature is too often condemned or neglected. There is genuine education in all æsthetic power, even in the lower form of appreciation of the ludicrous, the power to observe fine distinctions of incongruity. We say a thing is perfectly ludicrous, perfectly grotesque, and thereby recognize the art idea, namely, perfection in execution. Man is always striving to attain the perfect in some form, and the art idea is one of the highest in the field of education. Art leans toward the side of feeling, but is none the less rich and valuable for that. Shakespeare furnishes some of the highest types of art in literature. The flow of his verse, the light beauty of his sonnets, the boldness and wonderful aptness of his metaphors, the skill of his development, the ever-varying types, the humor, the joys, the sorrows, the wisdom, the folly of men, the condensation of events and traits and experiences in individual types, the philosophical and prophetic insight, the artistic whole of his plays, constitute a rich field of education.

The Gothic cathedral, with its pointed arch, its mullioned window, tapering spire, and upward-running lines, indicating the hope and aspiration of the middle ages, with its cruciform shape, typical of the faith of the Christian, is more than the stone and mortar of which it is constructed. The truly educated man in art perceives the adaptation, polish, and perfection in literature; discovers the grace, the just proportions, the ideal form and typical idea in sculpture; views the expression, grouping, sentiment, coloring, and human passion in painting; enjoys the harmonies, movements, and ideas in music, that combination of effects that makes subtile and evasive metaphors; discovers the conventionalized forms and mute symbols, the "frozen music" of architecture; finds grandeur in the mountains, glory in the sunset, metaphors of thought in every form of nature; laughs with the morning breeze, finds strength in the giant oak, and sorrow in the drooping willow.

We need the ideal. Let us not permit the mortal body to lord it too much over the immortal spirit. The ideal man is the purpose of education and the aim of existence, or life is not worth living. All material prosperity is naught except as contributing to that end. Sympathetic spirits are calling for more enlightenment and enjoyment, and leisure for the laboring classes. They believe that men should be men as well as machines, and that, if they are educated ideally, the practical will take care of itself. If we retain our belief in the high possibilities of the human soul, we shall have faith in ideal education, and shall confidently offer every opportunity for the highest development possible of the child's power for knowledge, enjoyment, and action. And let his development be full and rounded. Let the roar of ocean and the sough of the pines make music for his ears as well as the whir of factories; let the starry heavens speak to his soul as vividly as the electric lamp to his eye. Let us evolve from the material present ideals that shall stand in place of the vanished ones.

ELEMENTS OF AN IDEAL LIFE.

I.

THE MODERN GOSPEL OF WORK.

Philosophy of work—Some exemplars—Modern romance—Work for others—The complete man—Epic and idyl.

A gentleman who had resided some years in Central and South America, conversing one evening with friends upon a doctrine of happiness, illustrated his argument with an anecdote. A Yankee living in South America observed that the native bees had no care for the morrow. He thought to make a fortune by bringing hard-working honey bees from the North to this land of perennial flowers, where they could store up honey the year around, and he tried the experiment. The bees worked eagerly for a time, but soon discovered that there was no winter in this paradise, and they perched on the flowers and trees and dozed the livelong day. Our philosopher assumed that the indolent, improvident life of the ignorant natives of sunny climes is the one of real happiness, and that a life of great activity is not to be desired. If his theory holds, then the savage under his palm tree is happier than the civilized man of the temperate zone, the monkey in the tropical jungle is better off than the savage, and the clam is happiest of all.

An observant traveller, returning by the southern route from California, studies Indians of various tribes at successive stages of the journey. Near the Mohave desert he sees abject beings loafing about the railway station to beg from the curious passengers; further east he sees self-respecting red people offering for sale pottery or blankets—their own handiwork; later he notes members of another tribe working on railroad construction by the side of white laborers; as he approaches the settled region he observes yet others who have homes and farms and engage in civilized industry, and his thought runs along the ascending scale of being until he contemplates the highest energy of the most cultured and forceful minds of our best civilization. He instinctively decides that the desirable life is on the upper scale of intelligence, feeling, and action.

Happiness through work is the creed of the dawning century. The romance of chivalry gives place to the poetry of steam; democracy is teaching wealth and position the dignity of labor; evolution and psychology show action to be the consummate flower of thought and feeling; recent literature illustrates the gospel of effort; and religion reaffirms the doctrine that faith without works is dead.

Herbert Spencer's philosophy defines life to be "the continuous adjustment of internal relations to external relations." This adjustment implies self-activity. If man has been evolved through a long period of change, he is a survival of the fittest in the struggle for existence. His ancestral history is one of exertion, his powers have been developed by use, he maintains himself by striving, his normal state is in the field of labor, and logically it is there his welfare and happiness are found.

Max Nordau wrote a book on "Degeneration." It contains much interesting matter, many wholesome suggestions, and considerable false theory. He claims that the demands of modern civilization place men under too great a strain, that the human race is tending toward insanity, and that by and by we shall stop our daily newspapers, remove the telephones from our homes, and return to a life of greater simplicity. It is true that tension never relaxed loses its spring, and worry kills, but the most potent causes of degeneration are false pleasures and lack of healthful work. Evolution's most important ethical maxim is that deadheads in society degenerate as do parasites in the lower animal kingdom. Every idler violates a great law of his being, which demands that thought and feeling shall emerge in action. Every class of people has its idlers, men who desire to possess without earning. The aimless son of wealth and the tramp tread the same path. Universal interest in honest, healthful employment would cure nearly all the evils of society and state. Manual labor is the first moral lesson for the street Arab and the criminal, and the best cure for some species of insanity. True charity does not give when it can provide the chance to earn. Idlers, lacking the normal source of happiness, seek harmful pleasures, and learn sooner or later that for every silver joy they must pay in golden sorrow. False stimuli, false excitement, purposeless activities, take the place of vocation. Tramps are not the only vagabonds; there are mental and moral vagabonds whom a fixed purpose, a definite interest and principles of conduct would turn from degeneration to regeneration. Balzac, with his keen analysis, describes the career of a graceless spendthrift who, finally weary of himself, one day resolved to give himself some reason for living. Under good influences he took up a life of regularity, simplicity, and usefulness, and learned that men's happiness and saneness of mind are proportionate to their labors. This is the great lesson of Goethe's "Faust," set in imperishable drama for the instruction of the ages. Balzac's Curé of Montegnac speaks to a repentant criminal: "There is no sin beyond redemption through the good works of repentance. For you, work must be prayer. The monasteries wept, but acted too; they prayed, but they civilized. Be yourself a monastery here." Repentance, prayer, work—these are the way of salvation.

Every man of broad mind has full regard for the problems of labor and has faith in a progress that shall mean better conditions for the less fortunate, but Edwin Markham's "Man With the Hoe," as applied, not to special and extreme conditions of hardship, but in general to the problems of the human race, is wrong at the foundation; it is neither correct science, good philosophy, nor accurate history. It is the doctrine of the fall of man rather than of the ascent of man; it is the doctrine that labor is a curse. Without the hoe the human race would be chimpanzees, savages, tramps and criminals. In human development no useful labor ever "loosened and let down the brutal jaw" or "slanted back the brow" or "blew out the light within the brain" or deprived man of his birthright. At a stage of his progress, by cultivating the soil man of necessity cultivates his soul. The hoe has been an indispensable instrument to the growth of intelligence and morals, has been the great civilizer—a means of advance toward Plato and the divine image. Hardship may arrest development, but seldom causes degeneration. Our problem is not to free from bondage to work, but to relieve of burdens that are too heavy, and place a larger part on the shoulders of the strong and selfish.

Our educational philosophy at times wanders in dangerous bypaths, but there is a recent return to the plain highway. Some late notable utterances maintain that character must be formed by struggle, that a good impulse must prove its quality by a good act, that education is self-effort, and that passive reception of knowledge and rules of conduct may make mental and moral paupers. Here is an apt thrust from a trenchant pen: "Soft pedagogics have taken the place of the old steep and rocky path to learning. But from this lukewarm air the bracing oxygen of effort is left out. It is nonsense to suppose that every step in education *can* be interesting. The fighting impulse must often be appealed to."

I like to discover philosophy in the literature of the day, literature which does not rank as scientific, but contains half-conscious, incidental expression of deep perceptions of human nature. Kipling at his best sounds great moral depths, and teaches the lesson of life's discipline. He has a plain message for America as she takes her new place in the congress of the world. Civilized nations must take up the burden of aiding less favored peoples, not for glory or gain, but as an uncompromising duty without hope of appreciation or reward. We must expect the untaught races will weigh our God, our religion, and us by our every word and act in relation to them. We, as a nation, may no longer wear the lightly proffered laurel, but must expect the older, civilized nations will judge us by our wisdom, equity, and success in discharge of our new responsibilities. In Kipling's "McAndrew's Hymn" many years of hardship, sternly borne in obedience to duty, atone for misspent days under the influence of the soft stars in the velvet skies of the Orient. In "The 'Eathen" the author refers to the native inhabitants of India, whose most familiar household words are "not now," "to-morrow," "wait a bit," and whose chief traits are dirtiness, laziness, and "doin' things rather-more-or-less." He describes the raw English recruit, picked out of the gutter, recounts the stages of discipline that make him a good soldier, and finally a reliable non-commissioned officer—a man that, returned to his country, would prove a good and useful citizen.

"The 'eathen in 'is blindness bows down to wood 'an stone.
'E don't obey no orders unless they is 'is own;
'E keeps 'is side arms awful: 'e leaves 'em all about,
An' then comes up the regiment an' pokes the 'eathen out.
*   *   *   *   *
The 'eathen in 'is blindness must end where 'e began,
But the backbone of the Army is the non-commissioned man."

"L'Envoi" of "The Seven Seas" suggests the creed of a healthy soul: to accept true criticism; to find joy in work; to be honest in the search for truth; to believe that all our labor is under God, the Source of all knowledge and all good.

Robert Louis Stevenson is great as a novelist; he is greater in his brief writings and his letters. He presents some plain truths with attractive vigor. He says: "To have suffered, nay, to suffer, sets a keen edge on what remains of the agreeable. This is a great truth, and has to be learned in the fire.... In almost all circumstances the human soul can play a fair part.... To me morals, the conscience, the affections, and the passions are, I will own frankly and sweepingly, so infinitely more important than the other parts of life, that I conceive men rather triflers who become immersed in the latter. To me the medicine bottles on my chimney and the blood in my handkerchief are accidents; they do not color my view of life.... We are not put here to enjoy ourselves; it was not God's purpose; and I am prepared to argue it is not our sincere wish.... Men do not want, and I do not think they would accept, happiness; what they live for is rivalry, effort, success. Gordon was happy in Khartoum, in his worst hours of danger and fatigue."

A cartoon of Gladstone, appearing soon after he had ostensibly retired from public life, showed him, with eager look and keen eye, writing vigorous essays upon current political questions. It recalled the grandeur of a life filled with great interests, sane purposes, and perpetual action. Biography is the best source of practical ideals; it is philosophy teaching by example; the personal element gives force to abstract truths. Luther's Titanic power and courage under the inspiration of a faith that could remove mountains has served the purpose of millions of men in great crises.

Were I to seek an epic for its power to influence, I would go to real history and choose the life of William the Silent. For thirty years this Prince of Orange stood for civil and religious liberty in the Netherlands, in an age when men little understood the meaning of liberty. He sacrificed wealth and honors for his country. In spite of reverses, of the cowardice and disloyalty of his followers, of ignorance of the very motives of his action, he persevered. Throughout the long struggle he was hopeful, cheerful, and courageous. When the celebrated ban appeared, barring him from food, water, fire, shelter, and human companionship, setting a price on his head, in reply he painted in vivid colors a terrible picture of the oppressors of his people and held it up to the view of the civilized world. The motives which sustained him were faith in God, a strong sense of duty, and a deep feeling of patriotism. His biographer says: "As long as he lived he was the guiding-star of a whole brave nation, and when he died the little children cried in the streets."

Heine, the poet and philosopher, was dying in an obscure attic in Paris. He was wasted to a skeleton and was enduring the extremity of human suffering. He could see only dimly, as through a screen. As he himself said, there was nothing left of him except his voice. Under these almost impossible conditions, he was still laboriously writing, that he might leave a competence to his wife. A friend of his earlier days visited him, and through a long conversation his words sparkled with wit, humor, poetry, and philosophy. Surely the active spirit is more than the body! There was a feudal knight who went about saying to all despondent wayfarers, "Courage, friend; the devil is dead!" and he always spoke with such cheerful confidence that his listeners accepted the announcement as good news, and gained fresh hope.

In this Philosophy of Work is there no place for romance? Shall there be no thrilling adventure, nothing but dull duty and drudgery? Shall we have only dead monotony—no color, light, or shadow? Shall Carlyle's "splendors high as Heaven" and "terrors deep as Hell" no longer give a zest to life? Stevenson's "Lantern Bearers" has an answer for this natural and ever recurrent question. In a little village in England, along the sands by the sea, some schoolboys were accustomed to spend their autumn holidays. At the end of the season, when the September nights were black, the boys would purchase tin bull's-eye lanterns. These they wore buckled to their waists and concealed under topcoats. In the cold and darkness of the night, in the wind and under the rain, they would gather in a hollow of the lonely sand drifts, and, disclosing their lanterns, would engage in inconsequential talk. In his words: "The essence of this bliss was to walk by yourself in the black night; the slide shut, the topcoat buttoned; not a ray escaping, whether to conduct your footsteps or to make your glory public: a mere pillar of darkness in the dark; and all the while, deep down in the privacy of your fool's heart, to know that you had a bull's-eye at your belt, and to exult and sing over the knowledge.... Justice is not done to the versatility and the unplumbed childishness of man's imagination. His life from without may seem but a rude mound of mud; there will be some golden chamber at the heart of it, in which he dwells delighted; and for as dark as his pathway seems to the observer, he will have some kind of a bull's-eye at his belt.... The ground of a man's joy is often hard to hit. The observer (poor soul, with his documents!) is all abroad. For to look at the man is but to court deception. We shall see the trunk from which he draws his nourishment; but he himself is above and abroad in the green dome of foliage, hummed through by winds and nested in by nightingales. And the true realism were that of the poets, to climb up after him like a squirrel, and catch some glimpse of the heaven for which he lives. And the true realism, always and everywhere, is that of the poets: to find out where joy resides and give it a voice far beyond singing. For to miss the joy is to miss all. In the joy of the actors lies the sense of any action, that is the explanation, that the excuse. To one who has not the secret of the lanterns, the scene upon the links is meaningless. And hence the haunting and truly spectral unreality of realistic books." This quotation needs no excuse. The mould of human nature from which this copy was taken is forever broken, and can never be reproduced.

To be a lantern-bearer on the lonely heath, to rejoice in work and struggle—this is the romance, real, attainable, and apt for the world as it is and for the work we must do. If irrational pastime, attended with endurance, may be a joy, surely rational effort toward some desired result may have its poetry. Sacrifice and heroism are found in humble homes; commonplace labor has its dangers and its victories; and many a man at his work, in knowledge of the light concealed, the interest he makes of his vocation, his romance, exults and sings.

The world is as we regard it. Many look at the world as Doctor Holmes' squint-brained member of the tea-table views the plant kingdom. He makes the underground, downward-probing life of the tree the real life. The spreading roots are a great octopus, searching beneath instinctively for food, while the branches and leaves are mere terminal appendages swaying in the air. It is a horrible conception, and we are pained at standing on our heads. The tree roots itself to the earth and draws its nourishment therefrom that it may spring heavenward, and bear rich fruit and be a thing of beauty, a lesson and a promise. Man is rooted to the earth, but his real life springs into the free air and bathes in the glad sunlight.

The purpose of our labor determines its qualities of truth and healthfulness. Satisfaction must be sought by employing our faculties in the useful arts and in the search for truth. Perfection of self is the ultimate good for each individual, but this is attained, not in isolation, but in social life with its mutual obligations. The lesson of civil and religious liberty, taught by the great reformers, has been only partly learned. Individualism, rightly understood, is the true political doctrine, but the selfishness of individual freedom is the first quality to develop. Concerning great public questions often the attitude is as expressed in Balzac's words: "What is that to me? Each for himself! Let each man mind his own business!" Democracy is the way of social and political progress, but we have not yet reached the height of clear vision. We are struggling up the difficult and dangerous path, looking hopefully upward, thinking we see the summit, only to find at each stage that the ultimate heights are still beyond. When kings are dethroned, the hope of democracy is to enthrone public conscience. Here is a picture of a condition occasionally possible in any state of America to-day. We will say there is some great public interest, not a party problem, involving the financial prosperity and the essential welfare of the state, and affecting its credit, honor, and reputation abroad. And—with some noble exceptions—perhaps not a minister in his pulpit, not an orator on his platform, not a newspaper with its great opportunity for enlightening the people and exerting influence, not an educator, not a college graduate, not a high-school graduate, not a business man, not a politician arises and says: Here is a common good imperilled, and I for one will give of my time, my energy, and, if need be, according to my ability, of my money in its support. So long as such a state of apathy concerning public questions may exist, there is something still to be desired for the ideals of democracy and for our methods of education.

The Platonic philosophy has largely inspired educational work, and must still furnish its best ideals. But emphasizing the worth of the individual to himself has created a false conception of social obligation. Culture for culture's sake has been the maxim, but I have come to believe that a culture which does not in some way reach out to benefit others is not of much value to the individual himself. Some one has aptly illustrated this view: probably the drone in the bee-hive, when he is about to be destroyed, would say, "I would like to live for life's sake, and would like to buzz a while longer for buzz's sake."

I would see young men and women go out into the world with a true democratic spirit, with a ready sympathy for all classes of people, and with a helpful attitude toward all problems of state and society. The work of any public institution of higher learning is a failure in so far as its graduates fail to honor the state's claim on them as citizens. The great principle of evolution is the struggle for life; there is another equally important principle, namely, the struggle for the life of others. Altruism, dimly disclosed away down on the scale of being, finally shines forth in the family and home in all of those social sentiments that make human character beautiful and noble. Society is the mirror in which each one sees himself reflected, by which each attains self-consciousness, and becomes a human being. From coöperation spring industries, commerce, science, literature, art—all that makes life worth living. If the individual owes everything to society, he should be willing in some small ways to repay part of the debt.

The great Bismarck, that man of iron and blood, not given to sentimentality, in fireside conversation repeatedly proclaimed that during his long and arduous struggle for the unification of Germany he was sustained by a sense of duty and faith in God. "If I did not believe in a Divine Providence which has ordained this German nation to something good and great, I would at once give up my trade as a statesman. If I had not the wonderful basis of religion, I should have turned my back to the whole court." Some one has said that the essence of pessimism is disbelief in God and man. Fear is a kind of atheism. Heine once said: "God was always the beginning and end of my thought. When I hear His existence questioned I feel a ghastly forlornness in a mad world." The inspiration of labor is faith in God, faith in man, faith in the moral order of the world, faith in progress. The religious man should have a sane view of life, should have convictions, and the courage of his convictions. He should believe that his work all counts toward some great purpose.

The impulse to reverence and prayer is an essential fact, as real as the inborn tendency to physical and mental action. Its development is necessary to the complete man. The religious nature obeys the great law of power through effort, and increases strength by use. He who by scientific analysis comes to doubt the value of his ethical feeling has not learned the essential truth of philosophy, namely, that a thing's origin must not be mistaken for its character.

Some tendencies of the best scientific thought of to-day, seen here and there, confirm this view of man's nature. Here are some fragments, expressed, not literally, but in substance: It is the business of science to analyze the entire content of human consciousness into atomic sensations, but there its work ends. The man of history, of freedom and responsibility, whose deeds we approve or disapprove, is the real man, a being of transcendent worth, aspiring toward perfect ideals; and the teacher must carry this conception of the child's nature into the work of education. It is a scientific fact that prayer is for the health of the soul. It is useless to theorize on the subject—men pray because it is their nature; they can not help it. Even if prayer does not change the will of God, at least it does change the will of man, which may be the object of prayer. The Christian experience shows that prayer is a communion of man's spirit with God, the Spirit. John Fiske affirms the reality of religion. He argues that the progress of life has been achieved through adjustment to external realities; that the religious idea has played a dominant part in history; that all the analogies of evolution show that man's religious nature cannot be an adjustment to an external non-reality. He says: "Of all the implications of the doctrine of evolution with regard to Man, I believe the very deepest and strongest to be that which asserts the Everlasting Reality of Religion."

In this message to students we have emphasized a particular ideal, namely, normal activity, because one's own effort and experience count most for growth and power.

"It was better youth
Should strive, through acts uncouth,
Toward making, than repose on aught found made."

Students are at an age when to them the roses nod and the stars seem to wink. Their mental landscape is filled with budding flowers, singing birds, and rosy dawns. Every one has a right to consider his own perfection and enjoyment, his own emotions. One is better for his healthful recreations, his aspirations and ideals, his perceptions of beauty and his divine communings—the sweetness and light of the soul. We can only ask that the main purpose and trend of life may be laborious and useful, even strenuous and successful.

Lowell wrote of the pioneers who settled New England that they were men

"Who pitched a state as other men pitch tents,
And led the march of time to great events."

The pioneers of this Commonwealth were men who here pitched a state as other men pitch tents, and are leading the march of time to great events. The age, America, offer great opportunities to educated young men and women. Use them with courage. King Henry IV. of France once gained a great victory at Arques. After the battle, as he was leading his troops toward Paris, he met one of his generals coming up late with a detachment of the army, and thus greeted him, "Go hang yourself, brave Crillon! We fought at Arques and you were not there," as though the greatest privilege in life were an opportunity to contend and win for one's self a victory.

A few years ago I went to Ayr, the birthplace of Burns. I visited the poet's cottage, walked by the Alloway Kirk where Tam o' Shanter beheld the witch dance, crossed the Auld Brig and wandered by the banks and braes o' bonny Doon—and it is a beautiful stream. I found myself repeating lines from "Tam o' Shanter," "Bonny Doon," "Scots Wha Hae wi' Wallace Bled," and from some of the sweeter and nobler songs of Burns. And I thought of the mission of the poet. The scenery in and about Ayr is beautiful, but there is many another region equally attractive. The people with whom Burns dwelt, his neighbors and friends, were commonplace men and women, knowing the hardships, the drudgery, the pettiness of life. And yet he so sang of these scenes and these people, so touched every chord of the human heart, that annually thirty thousand travellers visit Ayr to pay their homage at the poet's shrine. The poetic view of life is the right one. The poet sees the reality in the commonplace. Our surroundings are filled with wonderful and varied beauty when we open our eyes to the truth. Our friends and companions are splendid men and women when we see them at their worth. For happiness as well as success add poetry to heroism.

"The Inscrutable who set this orb awhirl
Gave power to strength that effort might attain;
Gave power to wit that knowledge might direct;

And so with penalties, incentives, gains,
Limits, and compensations intricate,
He dowered this earth, that man should never rest
Save as his Maker's will be carried out.

* * * * *

There is no easy, unearned joy on earth
Save what God gives—the lustiness of youth,
And love's dear pangs. All other joys we gain
By striving, and so qualified we are
That effort's zest our need as much consoles
As effort's gain. Both issues are our due.

* * * * *

Better when work is past
Back into dust dissolve and help a seed
Climb upward, than with strength still full
Deny to God His claim and thwart His wish."

II.

THE PSYCHOLOGY OF FAITH.

Question stated—Some latest views of evolution—Some grounds of faith—Poetic insight—The practical life.

Mark Twain quotes a schoolboy as saying: "Faith is believing what you know ain't so." This definition is turned from humor into seriousness by some modern thinkers when they charge immorality against all whose beliefs are not scientifically established on sufficient evidence. They look upon what they consider unwarranted beliefs as a species of lying to one's self, demoralizing to intellect and character. If no element of faith may anywhere be tolerated, these same thinkers should reëxamine their own foundations. The only thorough agnostic in history or literature, agnostic even toward his own agnosticism, is Charles Kingsley's Raphael Aben-Ezra. Let us listen to him. "Here am I, at last! fairly and safely landed at the very bottom of the bottomless.... No man, angel or demon can this day cast it in my teeth that I am weak enough to believe or disbelieve any phenomenon or theory in or concerning heaven or earth; or even that any such heaven, earth, phenomena or theories exist—or otherwise."

In a last analysis our very foundation principles rest on a ground of faith, and a clear knowledge of this fact may make us more humble in the presence of other claims on our belief. Whenever the adventurous philosophic mind gazes over the dizzy edge at the "bottomless," it draws back and gains a firm footing on the reality of conscious ideas. To abandon this is annihilation.

Years ago an old friend of mine, very worthy, but somewhat self-opinioned and truculent, in a discussion on religious thought exclaimed: "What! believe in anything I can't see, touch, hear, smell, taste? No, sir!" He represented the uneducated instinctive belief in the reality of the outer world as revealed through the senses; and he would have violently affirmed the reliability of the senses and the existence of material things. But philosophy shows these also to be of faith.

Had he been asked whether he had a knowledge of space and time and of certain indisputable facts concerning them, and whether he could see or hear these entities and intuitive truths, he would have paused to think. The axioms of mathematics would have been a veritable Socratic poser to him, and he would have withdrawn from his position—would have acknowledged some truths as more certain, by the nature and need of the mind, than the existence of matter.

The modern scientist for practical purposes postulates the existence of conscious ideas, of the outer material world, of space and time. He accepts axiomatic truths. He goes farther; he postulates the uniformity of nature, and the validity of his reasoning processes. He discovers natural laws, and propounds theories concerning them. He investigates the physical correlates of mental processes. He has his favorite hypotheses concerning phenomena that defy his powers of analysis. He shows the process of the world as a whole to be evolution.

So far we have no controversy and should have none, did not some eminent investigators in the field of natural science claim to have covered the entire realm of legitimate inquiry, and deny the right to raise further questions or entertain beliefs, however strongly they may be prompted by our very constitution, concerning the origin and end of things, the meaning of the world, and man's place in it. To the well-rounded nature, faith is not necessarily limited to the physical world, and the credulity implied in unwarranted denial is at least as unscientific as positive faith.

Human nature rebels against conclusions wholly discordant with its best instincts, and, in the light of the most recent data and speculation, begins anew a discussion as old as philosophy. The subject is all the more important, because the uneducated mind, misled by superficial catch phrases of materialism, fails to know the reverent spirit of true science.

Here is an illustration relating to the general theme. A prominent biologist puts this statement before the reading public: "There is no *ego* except that which arises from the coördination of the nerve cells." I might take the contrary of the proposition and reply: "There is an *ego* not adequately described by your 'colonial consciousness' theory." Regarding each position as dogmatic, perhaps mine is as good as the biologist's. As to evidence, he founds his belief on the general fact of evolution and specifically upon the functions, partly known, partly conjectured, of nerve cells in the brain. He has no knowledge that a unit-being called the *ego* does not exist. His is the faith of denial of something which from his standpoint he can neither prove nor disprove. I also accept the facts of evolution and of the mechanism of the brain. I base my belief in the *ego* on certain views of other biologists, and on data of consciousness, morality, and religion, and the insight of all subjective philosophy. My faith is one of assent to something not admitting demonstrative proof. Have I sufficient reason for my faith in passing beyond the inductions of material science?

We present some latest views of eminent biologists. While evolution must be accepted as a fact, there is great uncertainty as to the factors that produce changes in the organic world. To-day there is small evidence that variations are produced by direct influence of environment. In the germ is the "whole machinery and the mystery of heredity." Since the microscope fails to reveal the causes, either of normal development or of variations, some are forced to accept, as the simplest and most rational hypothesis, the existence of a psychic principle in the germ. The facts appear to support the doctrine of purpose in evolution. So earnest and able a thinker as Professor LeConte frankly affirms: "With the appearance of Man another factor was introduced, namely, *conscious coöperation in his own evolution, striving to attain an ideal.*"

Professor Muensterberg is of high authority in experimental psychology and besides has a keen philosophic mind. His paper entitled "Psychology and the Real Life" is instructive and significant. He shows that it is the business of psychology to analyze the ideas and emotions, the whole content of consciousness, into sensations, to investigate the whole psychological mechanism, but that the primary reality is not a possible object of psychology and natural science. By his view it takes an act of free will to declare the will unfree; there can be no science, thought, or doubt that is not the child of duties; even skeptical denial demands to be regarded as absolute truth; there is a truth, a beauty, a morality independent of psychological conditions; psychology is the last word of a materialistic century, it may become the introductory word of an idealistic century. His views are maintained with force and power of conviction.

But these references are only incidental to the purpose of this discussion. They may serve to show (1) that science has no real proof against the dictum, "Evolution is God's way of doing things;" (2) that on the contrary it may support the spiritual view of the world; (3) that there are grounds of faith with which science properly has no business.

Evolution is according to nature's laws. Man is a product of evolution. Man possesses poetry and sentiment, conceives the beauty of holiness, and has speculative reason. None of these can properly be explained by merely materialistic evolution; they are not necessary to preservation of life. We have tried to wholly account for the ideals, emotions, and aspirations of human nature by analyzing them into primitive sensations and instincts. This is the fatal error of materialistic philosophy. The process of evolution is not analysis; it is synthesis, development, the appearance of new factors—a gradual revelation. It is our business to analyze, but, also, to try to understand the higher complex, the perfected product. The first stand of spiritual philosophy is faith in the validity of our own evolved being, and to this we have as much right as to faith in the reliability of our five senses.

The geologist might say: To me the grandeur of the mountain means nothing; I know how it was made. The cooling and contraction of the earth, the crushing and uplifting of strata, the action of air, wind, and water, the sculpturing of time, the planting of vegetation by a chance breeze—and you have your mountain, a thing of science. Yet Coleridge, standing in the vale of Chamounix and gazing on Mont Blanc,

> "Till the dilating Soul, enrapt, transfused,
> Into the mighty Vision passing—there,
> As in her natural form, swelled vast to Heaven,"

found it an emblem of sublimity, a voice from the throne of God. We shall find it hard to believe that the poetry of science can be explained on a merely physical basis. One may say: The religious sentiment means nothing to me; I know its origin; it is the result of bad dreams. A primitive ancestor, after a successful hunt, ate too much raw meat and dreamed of his grandfather. Thus arose the belief in disembodied spirits and a whole train of false conceptions. Yet we shall hardly grant that the religious feeling of the martyrs, which enabled the exalted spirit to lose the sense of unutterable physical torture, is adequately explained by the dream hypothesis.

A Beethoven string orchestra, to the musical mind, discourses most excellent music. It is a connected series of sublimated and elusive metaphors, arousing the harmonies of the soul, touching its chords of sweetness, purity, beauty, and nobility. Yet there are minds that find in it nothing—pardon the quotation—but the friction of horsehair on catgut. There are minds to which these grand mountains, this deep sky, these groves of pine are nothing but rock and vapor and wood. The elements make no sweet tones for them; they can not hear the music of the spheres. To them honor, courage, morality, beauty, religion, are but refined forms of crude animal instincts, by aid of which the race has survived in its struggle for existence. There are no soul harmonies—nothing but the beating of the primitive tom-tom. They believe nothing which can not be verified by the methods of physical science. They have no faith.

How many a man of science, on some slight hint pointing in a given direction, with faith and courage has pursued his investigations, adopting hypothesis after hypothesis, rejecting, adjusting, the world meanwhile laughing at his folly and credulity, until he has discovered and proclaimed a great truth. When in the world of mind we find phenomena calling for explanation, needs that can be met in only a certain way, higher impulses reaching out toward objects whose existence they prove and whose nature they define, shall we show less faith and courage because of some dogmatic view that there is no reality beyond the world of material existence? In this universe of mystery, anything may be supposed possible for which there is evidence, and any theory is rational that will best explain the facts. If we have not the sense to understand the deepest conceptions of philosophy, let us at least have the sense to stick to that common sense with which God has endowed us in order that we may know by faith the supreme truths concerning man.

Somewhere and somehow in the nature of things is an ideal that made us as we are—an ideal that is adequate to our nature, need, and conception. God at the beginning and God at the end of the natural world, and the world of consciousness seems a postulate that is necessary and warranted. Professor James writes of an old lady who believed that the world rests on a great rock, and that the first rock rests on a rock; being urged further, she exclaimed that it was rocky all up and down. Unless we postulate a spiritual foundation of things that is self-active and rational, we are no better off than the old lady. This appears to be a rational world, for it is a world that makes science possible; we believe it has a rational Creator.

We commonly account for our ideals as constructed in a simple, mechanical way; but the explanation will fail to satisfy the mind of artist or saint in his exalted moments when he has visions of perfection. He must conceive of a Being who possesses the attributes of perfect beauty and goodness. Belief in God consecrates man's endeavor to attain the highest standards. Without God the world has not a home-seeming for man. As in the dream in Vergil, always he seems to be left alone, always to be going on a long journey in a desert land, unattended.

Philosophy has spent much time and energy to discover the origin of evil; a saner quest would be the origin of good in the world. We know that in accounting for evil there is always an unexplained remainder—the righteous suffering, and the weak crushed under burdens too heavy. It may be that Spencer's age of perfection, seen away down the vista of evolution, will, when realized, not be inviting. Some one suggests that then men will be perfect, but perfectly idiotic. It is the great moral paradox that perfection must be obtained through struggle with imperfection. Laurels worn but not won are but a fool's cap. Freedom is possible only in a world of good and evil, a world of choice, and with freedom the humblest creature is infinitely above the most perfect mechanism made and controlled by a blind necessity. Cease to prate of a life of perennial ease under June skies; the divinity within us rises in majesty and will not have it so. After all, those who are overcome in the struggle may have their reward; at Thermopylæ the Persians won the laurels, the Spartans the glory.

Does evolution transform the nature of duty into a mere calculation of the sum of happiness? On the contrary, it adds to duty a practical way of discovering duties. Evolution affirms the truth that knowledge of right and wrong is a growth, and that new conditions bring new problems. The laws of nature and the organization of society promptly teach us applied ethics. True, we no longer search for eternally fixed codes; but whatever conduces to happiness and genuine welfare, whatever conduces to the beauty, dignity, and goodness of self and others is, as ever, a stern duty. It is not in the nature of man to bridge over the chasm between right, known as right, and wrong, known as wrong. The moral imperative, Turn toward the light, seek to see your duty and perform it, is "a presence which is not to be put by, which neither listlessness nor mad endeavor can utterly abolish or destroy."

"Faith means belief in something concerning which doubt is still theoretically possible," says a modern scientific writer. He continues: "Faith is the readiness to act in a cause the prosperous issue of which is not certified to us in advance. It is in fact the same moral quality which we call courage in practical affairs." We admire confidence and courage in the world of affairs, even when disaster may possibly follow. Have we not in our hearts the "substance of things hoped for, the evidence of things not seen," which constitute the faith of St. Paul? And shall we not use the courage of faith to seek a supreme good, when, though we do not find it, there is a reward even in the seeking? If I were to define faith I would call it the X-ray of the soul.

There can be no absolute break between old thought and new. The history of thought is a history of evolution. Modern science has not destroyed the old grounds of faith; it enables us to correct the beliefs built thereon. The next step of science will be a recognition and examination of subjective problems as such. When discarding old things, separate the treasure from the rubbish. If you have ceased to pray selfishly for rain, you need not deny the efficacy of prayer for change of heart, forgiveness of sins, and communion of spirit. If you cannot accept certain views of the Trinity, you need not reject the sublime Christian philosophy, or refuse to pay homage to the perfection of Christ. If you have discarded some doctrine of inspiration of the Bible, you need not deny or neglect the value of the divine ethical teachings of the Hebrews, or their grand sacred poetry—

> "Those Hebrew songs that triumph, trust or grieve,—
> Verses that smite the soul as with a sword,
> And open all the abysses with a word."

There is a faith which is a personal and conscious relation of man to God. It is said that in its true nature faith can be justified by nothing but itself. Here we enter the temple of the human heart and approach the holy of holies. This we do with reverent mien, even with fear and trembling. We quote from Prof. T. H. Green: "That God is, Reason entitles us to say with the same certainty as that the world is or that we ourselves are. What He is, it does not, indeed, enable us to say in the same way in which we make propositions about matters of fact, but it moves us to seek to become as He is, to become like Him, to become consciously one with Him, to have the fruition of his Godhead. In this sense it is that Reason issues in the life of Faith.... It is our very familiarity with God's expression of Himself in the institutions of society, in the moral law, in the language and inner life of Christians, in our own consciences, that helps to blind us to its divinity."

There is a poem, from an author not widely known, entitled "The Hound of Heaven." It will affect you according to the education, experience, and beliefs of each; but appeal to you it will, for in all is an insistent something that makes for righteousness.

> "I fled Him, down the nights and down the days;
> I fled Him, down the arches of the years;
> I fled Him, down the labyrinthine ways
> Of my own mind; and in the midst of tears
> I hid from Him, and under running laughter.
> Up vistaed hopes I sped;
> And shot, precipitated
> Adown Titanic glooms of chasmed fears,
> From those strong Feet that followed, followed after.
> But with unhurrying chase,
> And unperturbed pace,
> Deliberate speed, majestic instancy,
> They beat—and a Voice beat
> More instant than the Feet—
> 'All things betray thee, who betrayest Me.'"

The poem recounts a life made tragic by many a human error, but ever forced to listen to the following "Feet." It closes thus:

> "Halts by me that footfall:
> Is my gloom, after all.
> Shade of His hand, outstretched caressingly?
> 'Ah, fondest, blindest, weakest,
> I am He Whom thou seekest!

Thou dravest love from thee, who dravest Me.'"

To me it requires greater faith to call the Christian experience an illusion than to accept its reality and validity.

The true poet is the living embodiment of instinctive faith. His mind and heart are keenly alive to God's revelation of Himself in man and nature. He is a seer. His themes are the truths that come to him in visions from the realms of truth. He sees the principle of beauty in things; and familiar scenes, commonplace experiences are clothed in a spiritual glory. He accepts the world of facts and of science, but gives them their real meaning. Poetic insight, a thing so much contemned, because so little understood, is one of the best illustrations and evidences of the nature of faith. Wordsworth calls poetry "the breath and finer spirit of all knowledge."

A few months ago I chanced to be looking from a railroad train near Lake Erie in the very early dawn. I beheld, as I supposed, a beautiful expanse of water, with islands and inlets, and, beyond, a range of blue hills. I was lost in admiration of the view. As the light increased, a suspicion, at last growing into certainty, arose that I was the subject of an illusion, and that my beautiful landscape was but a changing scene of cloud and open sky on the horizon. But the blue hills still seemed real; soon they, too, were resolved into clouds, and only a common wooded country remained to the vision. The analogy to the dawn of civilization and the flight of superstition, and, finally, of faith, forced itself upon me, and I was troubled, seeing no escape from the application. Just then the sun arose, bringing the glory of light to the eye, and with it came a thrilling mental flash. There was the solution, the all-revealing light, the greater truth, without which neither the appearance of the solid earth nor of its seeming aërial counterpart would have been possible. Both evidenced the greater existence. Are not our fancies and our facts, our errors in the search of truth and our truths, our doubts and our faith, our life and activity and being, proofs of a Universal Existence—the revealer of truth, the source of truth, and the Truth?

This address has more than a formal purpose. Our beliefs in great measure determine our practical life. Freedom, God, and Immortality are conceptions that have ruled in the affairs of men and made the best products of civilization; they must still rule in the individual, if he would grow to his full stature. We are in a century of doubt, but I firmly believe that in the ashes of the old faith the vital spark still glows, and that from them, phœnix-like, will rise again the spiritual life in new strength and beauty.

Show your faith by your works; faith without works is dead. A mere philosophic belief in abstract ideals, not lived in some measure, may be worse than useless. A mere intellectual faith that does not touch the heart and brighten life and make work a blessing lacks the vital element. Follow your ideals closely with effort. Give life breadth as well as length; the totality will be the sum of your thought, feeling, and action. When the active conflict is over and the heroes recount their battles, may you be able to say: "I, too, was there."

There is still a practical side. Many young men have powers of growth and possibilities of success beyond their present belief; faith creates results. Every one has rare insights and rare impulses, showing his powers and urging him to action; it is fatal to ignore them. Faith is needed in business; confidence begets confidence. It is needed in social life; friendship demands to be met on equal terms. It is a ground of happiness; suspicion creates gloom and pessimism. It is needed for practical coöperation; suspicion is isolated. It is needed by the educator; faith and love make zeal in the calling. It is due even the criminal; in most men there is more of good than bad. Charity for the sins and misfortunes of humanity, hope for the best, faith in our endeavor must attend successful effort to aid men.

After all it is the essential spirit that one cultivates within him that will determine his manifold deeds. We can invoke no greater blessing than a character that in all ways will assert the highest dignity that belongs to a human soul. Be brave in your faith. When materialism, indifference, doubt, ease, and unseemly pleasure claim you for theirs (the Devil's own), let your answer be what is expressed in Carlyle's "Everlasting Yea": "And then was it that my whole *Me* stood up, in native God-created majesty, and with emphasis recorded its Protest: *I* am not thine, but Free!"

When I see some grand old man, full of faith, courage, optimism, and cheerfulness, whose life has conformed to the moral law, who has wielded the right arm of his freedom boldly for every good cause, come to the end of life with love for man and trust in God, seeing the way brighten before him, turning his sunset into morning, I must believe that he represents the survival of the fittest, that his ideals are not the mere fictions of a blind nature, serving for the preservation of his physical being, but that the order of his life has been in accord with realities.

III.

EVOLUTION OF A PERSONAL IDEAL.

Illustration and law of growth—Stationary ideals, Advance—Means of development—Be of to-day—A creed.

A famous artist once painted a portrait on a unique plan. He secured a copy of every photograph of the subject from his babyhood. When the painting was finished, there appeared in it the pictures of seven people of different ages, skilfully grouped and variously employed, but all portraits of the same person, each representing a stage of growth. We shall not attempt the work of the artist, but will endeavor to furnish the brush and colors, leaving you to fill in the sketches, now and at future times, at your leisure.

A tale is told of a man who awoke one night thinking of his past and groaning in evident mental distress. To the solicitous inquiry of his guardian angel, he replied: "I am thinking about the people I used to be." The angel, smiling, said: "I am thinking seriously about the people you are going to be"—thinking of

"The soul that has learned to break its chains,
The heart grown tenderer through its pains,
The mind made richer for its thought,
The character remorse has wrought
To far undreamed capacities;
The will that sits a king at ease.
Nay, marvel not, for I plainly see
And joy in the people you're going to be."

The gradual realization of higher and higher types is the general law of evolution in the organic world; it is also the process of the ideal spiritual development of the individual man. The potency of an infinitely varied and beautiful world was in the primeval mist. The potency of each higher type of being lies in the simpler form preceding. Ideally the potency of a soul of strength and beauty, of continuous development, is in the child and youth. The self of to-day is the material of possibility which should grow into the higher self of to-morrow.

Growth is not merely gain in knowledge and intellectual power. The science of education must include a vision of the entire human soul with its need of sympathy and direction, its vague dreams of possibility, its ideals half-realized. We must view the scale of feelings from the lowest animal instinct to the most refined ethical emotions, the order of their worth from the meanest vindictiveness to the highest altruism under God and duty, and note the struggle for the survival of the fittest of the impulses and motives under the guidance of reason and with the responsibility of freedom.

We see men, yet in the vigor of life, men of learning, of position, of opportunity, complacent in their attainments, fixed in ideas and methods adapted to a previous generation or a different environment, psychically prematurely old, their powers half-developed, their life work half-done. The men who reach the complete development of their powers constantly renew their youth, and march with modern events.

We see young graduates, men of power, who, through degenerate tendencies, lack of faith, lack of insight or lack of courage, remain stationary and satisfied in the grade to which their diplomas duly testify. They have as much life and growth and are as ornamental as a painted canvas tree in a garden. A lazy indifferent man once said he would as soon be dead as alive. When asked why he did not kill himself, he could only explain that he would as soon be alive as dead.

In the established church is sometimes observed by its devotees a special season of solitude and silence for religious meditation; it is called a "retreat." There is a German tale of an aged grandfather who, every Christmas season, spent a day alone in meditation upon the year and the years gone by, making a reckoning with himself, with his failures and his blessings, and casting a most conscientious account. On that day the noisy children were hushed by the servants—"The master is keeping his retreat"—and they went about in silent wonder and imagined he was making himself Christmas gifts in his quiet room upstairs. When he reappeared in the evening, after his day of solitude, he seemed by his quiet, gentle manners and thought-lit face to have received heaven-sent gifts.

I shall never forget the passage of Vergil which in my school days gave rise in me to a new sense of beauty in literature; nor shall I forget the unique and rich experience of the revelation. Every one has at times a new birth, a disclosure of hitherto unknown capacities and powers.

The soul must keep its retreats, not necessarily on church-anniversary days, but at epochs, at periods of dissatisfaction with the past, at stages of new insight—must have a reckoning with itself and readjust itself to life. When one reviews the panorama of his own history, and finds it inartistic, a profitless daub, empty of the ideal or heroic, he is keeping a retreat. When a new estimate of values and possibilities appears, he has experienced a conversion, has taken a new step in the evolution of his ideal life. The revolt of the soul may be as necessary to its health and growth as the upheaval of a nation is essential to its development. It is a battle for new principles, for advance, for freedom.

Tolstoï relates a most striking reminiscence of his own life, substantially thus: It was in 1872 that the Tolstoï of to-day saw the light. Then a new insight revealed his former life as empty. It was on a beautiful spring morning with bright sun, singing birds, and humming insects. He had halted to rest his horse by a wayside cross. Some peasants passing stopped there to offer their devotions. He was touched to the depths by their simple faith, and when he took up his journey he knew that the Kingdom of God is within us. He says: "It was then, twenty-three years ago, that the Tolstoï of to-day sprang into existence."

President Garfield, when at the head of Hiram College, once addressed his students, in a way that made a lasting impression, on the subject of "Margins." Personal distinction, success, depend, not on the average bulk of knowledge, power, and skill, but on that margin that extends a little beyond the reach of one's fellows, a margin gained by some extra devotion, by sacrifice and work, by ideals a little more advanced or more clearly seen.

Some recent and notable inductions of physiological psychology along the line of evolution reaffirm that without pain there can be no happiness, that without struggle there can be no positive character, that at times punishment may be most salutary and that a deadhead in society degenerates as does a parasite in the animal kingdom. Since these views are in line with the teachings of instinct and reason, from old Plato down, we may believe that evolution as applied to the spiritual nature of man is, indeed, becoming a hopeful doctrine. We have had somewhat too much of Herbert Spencer's pleasure theory, and pursuit of inclination, and the discipline of natural consequences, and lines of least resistance. The moral drama must be enacted on a field of conflict.

The principle of personal evolution is "ideals and action." Mr. Gladstone's wonderful character and great career are a pointed illustration of this fact. Even his fixed standards of conduct were a contribution to his growth and greatness. He always asked concerning a policy of state: Is it just? No unworthy motive was ever known to determine his public or his private acts. While working ever according to permanent standards of right, his was essentially a life of change and growth. Mr. Gladstone had a mind always seeking truth, and, moreover, had a rare capacity for receiving new ideas. In his history one can discover many distinct stages of development. He himself acknowledges three great "transmigrations of spirit" in his parliamentary career. He broke away from his early political traditions and, in consequence, more than once was obliged to seek new constituents who "marched with the movement of his mind." He was ever "struggling toward the light," and was ever a fighter. His political opponents said of him that his foot was always in the stirrup. His mind rested not by inactivity, but by "stretching itself out in another direction." He threw himself into new and important movements for humanity with tremendous zeal and force.

Lord Macaulay pithily expresses a law of human progress: "The point which yesterday was invisible is our goal to-day, and will be our starting post to-morrow." Maurice Maeterlinck says: "If at the moment you think or say something that is too beautiful to be true in you—if you have but endeavored to think or to say it to-day, on the morrow it will be true. We must try to be more beautiful than ourselves; we shall never distance our soul."

In the problem of growth do not neglect Emerson's principle of compensation. As men injure or help others, so they injure or help themselves. Punishment is the inseparable attendant of crime. Requital is swift, sure, and exact. Vice makes spiritual blindness. The real drama of life is within. Some one has said that punishment for misdeeds is not something which happens to a man, but something which happens in a man. Balzac describes a magic skin, endowed with power to measure the term of life of its possessor, which shrank with his every expressed wish. Personal worth grows or shrinks with the daily life and thought. Every one can will his own growth in strength and symmetry or can become dwarfed and degenerate. Wrong takes away from the sum of worth; virtue makes increase from the source of all good. Emerson says that even a man's defects may be turned to good. For instance, if he has a disposition that fails to invite companionship, he gains habits of self-help, and thus, "like the wounded oyster, he mends his shell with pearl."

If you would see the fulness of God's revelation in men, look into the minds of those whose biographies are worth writing—men who in affairs of the world have shown clear thought and accurate judgment, and in spiritual things have had visions that may strengthen and confirm your feeble faith. Study the record of their words spoken at the fireside in the presence of intimate and congenial friends, when they showed glimpses of the real self. Learn in biography the history of great souls and see in them the ideal which is the ideal of the race, and, hence, your ideal. With the going out of this century some great lives have ended—lives that embodied high types of rugged, honest satire, political power, poetic thought, pure statesmanship, ethical standards, religious faith, scientific devotion. Their histories have been written, and enough is in them to stir the semiconscious indolent nature of any young man to cultivate a high personal ideal. When I left college my first investment was in a few additional good books. I advise students to buy a few of the best biographies recently published, and read them with a reverent mind.

When you see a man of marked power, you may be sure, always sure, that he has used means of growth which average people ignore, means without which his strength would never have appeared. He has been a student, perhaps of Plato, of Shakespeare, of the Bible, of science or of human nature. He has gone deeply into the character or writings of master minds in some field of knowledge or activity. If he has a truly great nature he is able to find in many a passage of Hebrew writings a power that welled up from the great hearts of the prophets of old—or a wisdom that gradually evolved with civilization through experiment, disaster, struggle, and contrition, and was corrected and formulated with rare understanding by the few great minds of history. Such writings are a very wellspring of knowledge and understanding for a young man of this or any age.

Have you read the earlier as well as the later writings of Rudyard Kipling? What a growth of power! The evolution of his ideal ever promises and realizes greater things. When recently it seemed that the riper fruits of his progress would be denied us, the keenest solicitude was everywhere manifest. It was a spontaneous tribute to the principle of ideal spiritual evolution in the individual. We now know Kipling's secret. In his weakness and his sorrow he has already turned to a new and more ambitious undertaking and has gathered to himself all material that may enable him to pluck out from his subject the heart of its mystery, and reveal it to the world of thought and culture. It is with the magic of industry that he evolves the ideal of his life.

The following story is told of Kipling—that it is not authentic does not rob it of its use: Father and son were on a voyage. The father, suffering from seasickness, had retired to his cabin, when an officer appeared and cried: "Your son has climbed out on the foreyard, and if he lets go he'll be drowned; we cannot save him." "Oh, is that all?" replied Mr. Kipling; "he won't let go."

Be men of to-day; the past is useful to make us wise in the present. The poet Tennyson had a wonderful influence in his generation. His influence is due not alone to his rich thought and poetic skill; he had the broad liberal view that could adapt itself to the changing world of science, philosophy, and religion, and he thus opened up the avenues of approach to all classes of thinkers. He was a man with an evolving ideal, a free, sane, healthy mind.

Poetry is not a thing of the past; it has not yet become familiar with its new themes. Kipling can sing the "Song of Steam" and write the romance of the "Day's Work"—can find poetry in a locomotive, a bridge, a ship or an engine. Kipling is right when he makes McAndrew, the hard-headed engineer of an ocean liner, see in the vast motor mechanism an "orchestra sublime," "singing like the morning stars," and proclaiming: "Not unto us the praise, or man." "From coupler-flange to spindle-guide I see Thy Hand, O God"—and this vision is always the ultimate ground of poetry. On a palace steamer between New York and the New England coast I once heard an uncultured workman exclaim: "When I watch this mighty engine, with its majestic, powerful movement, I feel that there is a God." At first thought the sentiment was humorously illogical, but his instinct was right. The works of nature and the works of man alike suggest a divine origin—God working in nature and working through man.

If this is a divine world, then there is no claim of the commonplace, no form of daily labor, no need of the unfortunate, no problem of society or government that is not a theme of dignity and worthy of attention and helpful effort. The form of truth is an empty, useless abstraction, unless it is given a content, unless it adjusts wrongs, removes evils, improves material conditions, and strengthens growth among all classes of people to-day. The man who beautifies his lawn, plants trees, lays good walks or cleans the streets is made more conscious of the divine within him—is a better man. Spinoza regarded his skill in making lenses to be as essential a part of his life as his philosophical interest.

Every advance in civilization changes the perspective, and new views and truths appear. Within a few years we have seen in America almost an entire change of attitude regarding many essential political and social questions. Throughout the world, Christianity, by clearer interpretation of its spirit, is gaining new influence in practical fields. New problems have not the enchantment of distance; history and poetry have not thrown a halo about them; but they have the interest of present, practical, living issues. Every great man has attained his self-realization as a creative factor in the work of his own age. Take a hand in making current history.

Successful men have shown at the close of their student life only the hope of what they finally became. But they were men who knew how to cherish every helpful impulse, to learn from every experience, to profit by each fresh insight, to concentrate their powers upon single tasks, and at each fulfilment look forward to still greater undertakings. Such minds wear the beauty of promise,

> "that which sets
> The budding rose above the rose full blown."

The realization of ideal promise is not merely intellectual power and practical attainment. A man may have these, and yet lack a rich mind. Sympathy, pure ideals, morality, religious sentiment belong to a complete nature. Without them one is not a fit leader or a choice companion. A wholly irreligious man is not conscious of his soul. As the years advance, with the progressive man there is more heart, more simplicity and truth, more moral and spiritual interest.

In the "Memoir of Lord Tennyson" by his son, a chapter on the "In Memoriam" throws brilliant side lights on the essential character of the great poet. One would almost take the truths there expressed as his creed, and the inner life there revealed as the consummation of a personal ideal. We note his "splendid faith in the growing purpose of the sum of life, and in the noble destiny of the individual man;" his belief that "it is the great purpose which consecrates life;" his feeling that "only under the inspiration of ideals, and with his 'sword bathed in heaven,' can a man combat the cynical indifference, the intellectual selfishness, the sloth of will, the utilitarian materialism of a transition age;" his faith that "the truth must be larger, purer, nobler than any mere human expression of it;" his affirmation that, if you "take away belief in the self-conscious personality of God, you take away the backbone of the world." He believed in prayer. In his own words: "Prayer is like opening a sluice between the great ocean and our little channels when the great sea gathers itself together and flows in at full tide."

Ideals do not belong to a mystical realm, to a remote age or to an indefinite future. They are not the exclusive possession of sage, saint, or poet. They belong to this day, here, to us. They belong to the professional man, as a man, as much as to the man of liberal culture.

To see the idyllic in what is familiar, to realize the heroic in ourselves, to make the lessons of greatness our own, to work with the spirit of our time are the means of growth. Every thought and every act, flowing from the conscious will, fashion the soul.

> "I held it truth, with him who sings
> To one clear harp in divers tones,
> That men may rise on stepping-stones
> Of their dead selves to higher things."

IV.

THE GREEK VIRTUES IN MODERN APPLICATION.

Essential conditions for a satisfactory life—A sound body—Courage—Wisdom—Justice—Reverence—The practical world.

At the risk of imitating the severe logical discourses which proceed at least as far as fifthly, let us enumerate some essential conditions that by the agreement of thoughtful men are requisite for a satisfactory life: (1) a sound body; (2) courage; (3) intellectual ideals; (4) moral ideals; (5) reverence. While these elements are selected for their intrinsic value, without reference to the history of ethical thought, the discovery that they show more than a fancied similarity to the ancient and the early Christian ideals strengthens our belief in their value, and suggests that essential human standards are not for one people or one age, but for all peoples and all time, and that they are spontaneously recognized even in an age like ours, when men readily turn toward utilitarian ends.

If we go back to the dawn of philosophic thought and listen to the early revelators of the nature of man and his relation to the world and society—converse with Plato in the groves of Academus, or walk with Aristotle in the shady avenues of the Lyceum—we find them proclaiming the great truths which have been confirmed by the experience of ages, and urging upon men Moderation, Courage, Wisdom, Justice, and the Good, or God, as aim. If we cross over from the ancient world to the Christian Empire, where old ethical thought was already taking on deeper meaning, broader application, and richer life, we find in the Cardinal Virtues of St. Ambrose and St. Augustine a new and vitalized form of the Greek Virtues: Temperance, Christian Fortitude, Christian Wisdom, Christian Justice, God as aim. If we come down to modern times, and catch the spirit of ideals that still dwell among the people, we find that human nature is everywhere the same, and that the experience of human life in all ages discovers through the organization of society the same divine principles—laws to be reverenced and obeyed, to be followed as practical guides to success.

Modern psychology has rendered a service of far-reaching practical benefit in showing more definitely the intimate connection between the brain and mental action. In this connection of body and soul the two are correlated; the brain is organic to the functions of the soul. The health of the brain is largely dependent upon general physical conditions, and the old apothegm, *"Mens sana in corpore sano,"* is interpreted with a new meaning not fully known in the days of Juvenal.

Maxims of health, sifted by the experience of ages, transmitted from generation to generation, and confirmed by the proofs of modern science, are wisdom of inestimable value for our instruction. He who wastes energy of the body wastes vigor and duration of mental power. Rev. William R. Alger used to say: "Keep yourself at highest working capacity by preserving the vigor of the body." The various ways of wasting physical energy are susceptible of classification, and it is well worth the while to make a thoughtful analysis of the subject. We admire the firm step, erect bearing, clear eye, and bright brain that belong to healthful habits and noble manhood. Many a man by carefully conserving the vital forces will outlive and outdo others who, with stronger bodies, waste their energy.

Physical sins react upon the mind and debase character. They are signs of a character already weak, and the interaction between mind and body doubly hastens the relaxing of just restraint. The ancient virtue of moderation, or temperance, meant more than temperate habit; it meant the submission of animal unreason to reason—the "observance of due measure in all conduct."

In accord with the maxims of health are the Greek Virtue of Moderation, the Cardinal Virtue of Temperance, the Hebrew Purity. Regard for these maxims is an important condition of success.

Courage appears in the Greek Category as heart for energetic action, and in the Cardinal Virtues as firmness for the right and against the wrong. Courage is the *sine qua non* of success. The student must have courage to overcome his inertia. A venerable professor of my college days used to say: "Every young man is naturally as lazy as he can be, and the greatest problem of education is to gain an energetic will." Courage is required to undertake an enterprise demanding long years of toil. A volume recently published contains the early experience of celebrated authors now living, and nearly every one owes his success to a persevering determination, in spite of poverty, rebuffs, criticism, and repeated failures. Their genius lies in their courage. We need the courage of our convictions to stand by the right. The great reformers have shared this kind of confidence of soul. Nearly all of Carlyle's types of the world's great heroes possessed it to an almost sublime degree, and, most of all, the hero of the Reformation. Waiving all religious controversies that centre about the doctrines of Martin Luther, he is a figure for the world to admire. Some of his memorable words are known as household words, but, like strains of familiar grand music, are ever grateful—they lose nothing by repeating. When warned that Duke George of Leipzig was his enemy he said: "Had I business, I would ride into Leipzig though it rained Duke Georges for nine days running." When summoned to the Diet at Worms, he answered the friends who would dissuade him: "Were there as many devils in Worms as there are roof tiles, I would on." When urged in the presence of that august council to recant, he replied: "Here I stand; I can do no other; God help me." And the courage of his religious faith rose to its climax when he boldly faced the supernatural and hurled his inkstand at the head of the Devil himself. The student needs the courage of faith in his own powers and possibilities. Many a one fails because he has not confidence in himself. In rare moments of meditation one sometimes discovers capacities and possibilities of attainment that become a life inspiration.

We are proud of our Teutonic ancestry; of the bold enterprise that led the Teutons across Europe in conquest, or impelled them to embark in their galleys and push forth with adventurous spirit, and fearlessly ride the tempestuous waves, as their oars kept time to the music of their songs of victory. Their courageous and progressive spirit, tamed and refined, reappeared in the religious convictions of the Puritans, in the settlement of America, in the westward march of civilization in our own country, in the confidence of the pioneers that early crossed the plains and pitched their tents by these mighty mountains, in the energy that has made all that the world holds as greatest and best in material civilization, invention, government, science, literature, and moral and religious principle. The young man who has in his veins the blood of this people, and inherits the blessings that his race has wrought out, is a recreant to his trust if he does not stand courageously for all that is best in his own development, and all that is best in the progress of his age. Thor, the Norse god, possessed a belt of strength by which his might was doubled, and a precious hammer which when thrown returned to the hand of its own accord. When he wielded the hammer, as the Northern legends relate, he grasped it until the knuckles grew white. This hammer is an heirloom of the Northern races, handed down from the Halls of Walhalla. And herein lies the secret of success: grasp the hammer until the knuckles grow white.

Plato held Wisdom to be the supreme means by which to attain the great purpose of human existence. The Cardinal Virtue of Christian Wisdom is to gain knowledge of God. Plato conceived growth in wisdom to be a gradual realization, in the consciousness of man, of the eternal ideas. Man came from heaven and in his progress in knowledge he was but climbing the upward path to regain his lost estate. The exercise of wisdom marked him off from the lower order of beings, and he was fulfilling the distinctively human function only when living a rational life.

If nature is a congeries of metaphors arranged in a system of relations and constituting a sublime allegory, and we, being the offspring of God, may interpret this allegory and thereby come to a consciousness of verities, if there is a spiritual sense that may feel the presence of great truths and of a personal God—then man pursues his supreme calling when through the laws of physical nature, when through the beauty of its forms, when through knowledge of self, when through the world's history and literature and philosophy he aims at a further acquaintance with truth. If knowledge and the power that comes through knowledge enhance our material civilization and make more favorable conditions for the body and more leisure for the mind and more refinement for the spirit, if to create material things brings us more in accord with the creative spirit of the universe, then we have the highest incentives to gain knowledge toward so-called practical ends.

The universities are not always the first discoverers of wisdom, but they are the storehouses of the wisdom of the ages, and the distributing points. They are not a substitute for nature and real life, but they help to interpret both. They are not a substitute for practical experience, but they bestow the instruments with which to do better the work of practical experience. They do not create power, but they develop power.

A few geniuses have in strong degree the intellectual impulse and follow it until they become original and creative, and contribute to the world's insight. But the average youth needs all that the formal training of the schools can give him. When the student is once aroused by the sense of his privileges and duties, he will select no easy goal to attain. He will not be satisfied until he has learned the secrets of nature's processes, has examined his own nature, has made use of the recorded experience of the ages—thereby taking a giant stride in knowledge that he could not have taken alone—has given himself the power to help in the work of his own time.

Justice was regarded by Plato as the ground of social uprightness; Christian justice recognized the brotherhood of man, with all that follows in moral conduct; "moral ideals" for us has the same significance. This is not the place for the discussion of ethical theories, but it is of the highest importance for the young man, after wandering more or less vaguely over the field of ethical doctrines, to turn to the nature of his own being and find there written the supreme fact of moral obligation, with its implications of freedom of will, a personal God, and immortality of the soul.

Every man knows that even in his ordinary approvable acts he does not work to the end of pleasure, but that he has impulses that reach out in fellowship and compassion toward others, impulses that reach out toward the Truth and Beauty and Supreme Goodness of the world. Every man knows that he possesses a power to choose amongst and regulate his impulses; that such aims are to be employed as will conduce to the perfection of his being and of all human being; that his reward lies in this perfection, in a noble and approvable character, which is not to be completed in this life, but is to attain its full realization in a future life. And hence is revealed to him the rational necessity of that life, without which the present struggle and growth would lack meaning.

If there is moral order in the universe, then man will be successful as he conforms to that order. If he goes against the great silent forces moving in the direction of Right, his life can but result in failure. Men who show a disregard for moral law are held to possess a dangerous malady slowly decaying the tissues of the soul. They are treated with suspicion in business relations and condemned in the minds of others and by their own judgment. Sound to the core must a man be who would make the most of life and receive the approval which the world bestows upon character.

A true man is bold; he feels that for him all the forces of right will contend. He has courage for his work, because he knows he is on the right path and is moving toward ever higher attainments and a supreme result.

The subject is old as man, the thoughts are trite; why not utter your maxim and proceed, or rather say nothing? While there are lives empty of purpose and hearts that bleed in contrition and tragedies that fill prisons and madhouses, there is much to say and more to do. Have we no further use for wisdom? Have we ceased to erect perennial monuments to the memory of saints and reformers? If the subject is old, the generations of men are new, and the race has not attained its perfection. The best men and the best thoughts reveal us to ourselves, are the source of our aspiration; and we of the present, not half-way toward the goal, have need of our Socrates, Augustine, Luther, and supremely of the divine Christ. We still have need of our Pilgrim's Progress.

The aim of Plato's philosophy was the Supreme Good, or God. The Cardinal Virtues were framed in the light of religious faith. Reverence is the sentiment whose object is God. Says the Sage of Chelsea: "All that we do springs out of Mystery, Spirit, invisible Force." Some, well-versed in Spencer's works, have failed to note this passage: "One truth must grow ever clearer—the truth that there is an Inscrutable Existence everywhere manifested, to which the man of science can neither find nor conceive either beginning or end. Amid the mysteries which become the more mysterious the more they are thought about there will remain the one absolute certainty, that he is ever in the presence of an Infinite and Eternal Energy, from which all things proceed." Add to this the Faith which is the "substance of things hoped for, the evidence of things not seen," and you have the origin of all religions, of all temples of worship. It is the conception of the philosopher and the insight of the poet; it is held most strongly by the most profound. Few great men, though they may reject formal creeds, are without the feeling of Reverence. Carlyle's "Everlasting Yea" is the vision of a true seer, and it reveals, in the spontaneous language of earnest thought, the breadth and depth of a possible Christian experience. He speaks through the hero of the "Sartor Resartus." By disappointment and dim faith the universe had become to him a vast merciless machine; he was filled with an indefinable fear. But over his soul came the spirit of Indignation and Defiance, and he shook off fear of all that is evil, and all that may happen of evil. In his words: "The Everlasting No had said: 'Behold, thou art fatherless, outcast; and the Universe is mine (the Devil's)'; to which my whole Me now made answer: 'I am not thine, but Free, and forever hate thee!'" This is but the first step, and only by the "Annihilation of Self" does he awake to a "new Heaven and a new Earth." Now nature is seen to be the "Living Garment of God." The Universe is no longer "dead and demoniacal," but "godlike and his Father's." He looks upon his fellow man with an "infinite Love, an infinite Pity," and enters the porch of the "Sanctuary of Sorrow." Happiness is no longer the aim; happiness cannot be satisfied. "There is in man a *Higher* than Love of Happiness; he can do without Happiness, and instead thereof find Blessedness!" "Love not pleasure; love God. This is the EVERLASTING YEA." The Temple of Sorrow (the Christian Temple) is partly in ruins, but in a crypt the sacred lamp still burns for him, and for all. Applied Christianity is action. He says: "Do the Duty which lies nearest thee: thy second Duty will already have become clearer." Thy opportunity is in whatever thy condition now and here offers thee. "Whatsoever thy hand findeth to do, do it with thy whole might." Christianity "flows through all our hearts and modulates and divinely leads them." Of immortality he says: "Know of a truth that only the Time-shadows have perished, or are perishable; that the real Being of whatever was, and whatever is, and whatever will be, *is* even now and forever.... Believe it thou must; understand it thou canst not."

If we may draw a lesson from this, Carlyle's greatest work, it is that the completeness of life requires vivifying, hope-giving, sin-subduing, courage-inspiring faith and reverence. To the hero of Carlyle's prose poem success did not come, until the "Fire-Baptism" of his soul. He confesses: "I directly thereupon began to be a man."

Are these ideals of value for practical success? Yes, for all the success worth striving for and worth having. Does not craft succeed better than honesty? Sometimes, and for a time, but honesty appears to be even the best policy, and it is the essential stamp of real manhood and womanhood. The genuine heroes of all history are the morally great. Are not such standards too high—impractical ideals for the pulpit and platform, which no one is expected to carry into real life? No one attains even his own ideals, much less the absolute standards; but they are the steady aim of a fully successful life.

If a young man is true to himself, the bounties of nature, the good will of others, the coöperation of the forces of right, and the approval of God are his. The world waits to see what he will do with his powers and opportunities. Much is expected of him, and rightly. The state which has helped educate him expects much; the home which has made sacrifices for him expects much. Will he have the courage to stand by his ideals? To progress must be part of his religion. When the oak has ceased to put forth its leaves and extend its branches, it has gone into hopeless decay. There is no lasting happiness but in action and ever new and higher realizations.

Longfellow represents early manhood turning regretfully from the memory visions of childhood and youth to the earnest work of life.

"Visions of childhood! Stay, O stay!
Ye were so sweet and wild!
And distant voices seem to say,
It cannot be! They pass away!
Other themes demand thy lay;
Thou art no more a child!

"The land of Song within thee lies,
Watered by living springs;
The lids of Fancy's sleepless eyes
Are gates unto that Paradise,
Holy thoughts, like stars, arise,
Its clouds are angel's wings.

* * * * *

"Look, then, into thine heart, and write!
Yes, into Life's deep stream!
All forms of sorrow and delight,
All solemn Voices of the Night,

That can soothe thee, or affright,—
Be these henceforth thy theme."

V.

THE STUDENT AS CITIZEN.

Hebrew and Greek standards of citizenship—Each a part of the whole—Responsibility of the scholar—The student's obligation to the state—Political standards.

Solomon, in the fulness of his wisdom and the maturity of his moral strength, wrote Proverbs. In the third chapter are many appeals in behalf of ideal manhood, and in behalf of justice and mercy in relations with one's fellow men. He exhorts men to depart from evil and hold fast to truth. He instructs them that intellectual and moral wisdom is better than silver and gold and rubies; that it gives long life, riches, power, and peace of mind. The wise shall find favor in sight of God and man. Reverence for God contributes to worldly success and the growth of character. With equal force he teaches regard for the rights and the welfare of others. "Devise not evil against thy neighbor." "Strive not with a man without a cause." "Choose not the ways of the oppressor." "Withhold not good from them to whom it is due, when it is in the power of thine hand to do it." And he sums up the whole matter in the sentence: "God blesseth the habitation of the just."

Men sometimes question whether ideals and Utopias have any practical value. Note the words of Professor Jowett, penned after he had spent years of his intense life in translating and commenting upon the Dialogues of Plato—writings which, in broad outlines, represent the best ideals of all philosophy for the individual and for society. He says: "Human life and conduct are affected by ideals in the same way that they are affected by the examples of eminent men. Neither the one nor the other is immediately applicable to practice, but there is a virtue flowing from them which tends to raise individuals above the common routine of society or trade, and to elevate states above the mere interests of commerce or the necessities of self-defense. Most men live in a corner, and see but a little way beyond their own home or place or occupation; they 'do not lift up their eyes to the hills;' they are not awake when the dawn appears. But in Plato, as from some 'tower of speculation,' we look into the distance and behold the future of the world and of philosophy. The ideal of the state and of the life of the philosopher; the ideal of an education continuing through life and extending equally to both sexes; the ideal of the unity and correlation of knowledge; the faith in good and immortality—are the vacant forms of light on which Plato is seeking to fix the eye of mankind."

In Plato's Ideal Republic the ruler is to be a man of wisdom and probity, and is to consider only the good of his subjects. "Until political greatness and wisdom meet in one, cities never will cease from ill." The citizen must perfect his calling, however humble, as an artist perfects his art, and must form a harmonious and useful factor in the state. States must be organized on the "heavenly," that is, the ideal, pattern. After developing the understanding of justice through the ten books of the "Republic," Socrates concludes: "Need we hire a herald, or shall I proclaim the result—that the best and the justest man is also the happiest, and that this is he who is the most royal master of himself; and that the worst and most unjust man is also the most miserable, and that this is he who is the greatest tyrant of himself and of his state."

The good citizen is described in Plato's "Laws" as he who honors his own soul, obeys the laws, meets the just demands of the state with endurance; who holds virtue above all other good, teaches children reverence, instead of bestowing upon them riches; who sets a good example, holds a contract as sacred, aids the suffering; who is trusted because of his truthfulness, does no injustice, exerts good influences, is ambitious without envy; who is gentle, forgives the penitent, loves not self unduly; who is cheerful and hopeful in misfortune; who is wise and moderate, and courageous in spirit.

Thus the wisdom of the Greek confirms the wisdom of the Hebrew, and, were we to trace the Christian teachings that constitute the true spirit of our modern civilization, we should find these same maxims, wrought out with fuller understanding, given a richer content and a broader application. The good citizen is he who is true to his best nature, and toward others is just, truthful, merciful, and helpful. It requires no new philosophy to solve the problems of society, only a better grasp and use of the old; for the germs of essential truths are as old as man, and have their origin in the mind of the Creator, who made this a moral world.

Each man, as a part of the universe, is subject to the universal will of God revealed in him; he, though a free agent, is under universal law, binding upon him as sharing in the common brotherhood. Did a different universe walk under your hat and under mine, then there would be no society, no brotherhood, no individual growth; so far as a man isolates himself in selfishness and narrowness, he is detached from the source and life of his being, and perishes by himself. He remains undeveloped, because the soul comes to know itself only by reflection in the mirror of kindred natures. The state is the organization that brings men into the most favorable conditions for the interplay of mind upon mind and heart upon heart.

As a part of the whole, each man must have his vocation. Man is conditioned by the needs of his physical being. He is compelled to make requisition on the fruitfulness of the earth, the abundance of the sea, and all the forces of nature. This demand upon his energies develops his intelligence and creative power. By serving his own needs he also serves others and contributes to a material civilization favorable to soul growth. The most favorable material conditions, however, are only the scene for the play of spiritual forces, and on this scene some find their special vocation in arousing and guiding mental and moral activities. He who, being able, does not contribute by his vocation to the common good, is a drain upon the whole; he takes without giving, and has no just share in the products of earth, the protection of state, or the favor of the Universal Father.

The ideal scholar is a man of rich thought and feeling, one who has realized much of his possibility, has come to a consciousness of universal truths. He has variety, breadth, and definiteness of knowledge, and, hence, is able more wisely to play his part in the state. He is the conservator and transmitter of the thought of the ages. From his acquaintance with the past he may interpret the present. By his own activity and invention he may add to the store of wisdom and the progress of civilization. He is able to view broadly the field of knowledge. He should judge wisely of events, and be able to sift useless details from essential truths. Upon him rests the responsibility of having many talents committed to his charge; he must gain other talents.

But this educated power is not to be merely self-centred. In these days no man is privileged to live an unproductive life. The development of his nature and the enjoyment of his powers is every man's right; but mere serene pleasure in exalted thought and feeling, as sought by the mediæval recluse, in an age when ideals must be followed by action, when utility is yoked to philosophy, is no longer tolerable in scholar or saint. The world demands the best expression of every man's best ability. The educated man should be a man of action and influence. If he chooses literature, he must give mankind the result of his deepest insight. If he chooses science, he enters a vast field, and the world expects of the trained specialist some fresh contribution to knowledge or skillful application in using the forces of nature. If he chooses teaching, he holds his only valid commission from the wise men of all ages. He is a mediator between the whole world of intellectual and moral wisdom and the needs of the plastic mind, and he is in large degree responsible for the shape it assumes and its beauty and worth. Young minds will reflect the richness or poverty of the thought, feeling, and life of the teacher. College-trained educators have a greater responsibility in proportion to their superior advantages. In whatever field, the educated man must use his trained powers for the honor of his calling.

The world has special claims upon the learned professions. The client pays for the honest service of the advocate, and, to the full limit of the justice involved, he may demand the best effort of his patron. The graduate in medicine has a mission, not alone of drugs and instruments, but of ministering to the mind diseased. His relations call for the soul of honor and delicacy and secrecy. The nature of his profession requires the most devoted service.

This demand for unselfish public service from the educated has not merely an objective significance. A man's full growth is, in a large measure, dependent upon the effective outward expression of his better self. Man finds his well-being in regard for the well-being of others.

There are times when the popular clamor of those who see only the near event must be resisted by the steady courage of citizens of far-reaching vision. One such man may see a truth more clearly than a thousand of average judgment. Plato surpassed the race in discovery of the foundations of truth. Copernicus penetrated to the centre of the solar system, and, there taking his stand, all the orbs moved before him in harmony. Such a standpoint, amid all the complexities of affairs, is always to be sought by men of deep discernment.

He who is educated by society or by the state stands under a peculiar obligation. The state says: I offer you as your right the best opportunities for your development; I provide for the acquisition of professional and mechanical skill. As a human being, for whom I am responsible, you have a claim to these privileges; but I give them also for the further welfare and progress of the whole, and I demand that you use your opportunities appreciatively and wisely. I expect you to conserve your physical being, to develop your powers, to train your mind for service and your heart to regard the claims of society. I expect no dwarfed and distorted growth, but a growth that has expanded in normal beauty and strength. The state has trained you that you may be an active factor for the welfare and glory of the state—a factor that shall consider the state's problems, shall take part in political affairs, shall occupy honestly positions of responsibility, shall stand for the right and raise its voice vigorously for every just cause, shall impart of its knowledge and professional skill in proportion to the full measure that has been received. Good to the state is the state's due; withhold not that good when it is in the power of your hand to do it. If your power is used selfishly, if your cunning is turned to the harm of your foster mother, if your influence leads men aside from the path of moral progress, I disown you as unworthy and ungrateful, and unconscious of your obligations as a man and a citizen.

The name of a country stands for more than its territory, people, and government. It represents the principles and conditions that gave it birth, the battles in defence of its integrity and honor, the civil conflicts for the triumph of the best elements, the monuments to the loyalty and sacrifice of its founders, defenders, and preservers. It represents the glory of its heroes, statesmen, poets, and seers; it stands for the peculiar genius and mission of the people. It is a heritage whose glory is to be maintained by the character, wisdom, and devotion of all its citizens.

I do not take the pessimistic view of political life. Men in places of responsibility are more disposed toward the right than is allowed by their political opponents. Respect is due to our rulers, and a man is not to be charged with wrong motives merely because his judgment is not in accord with ours, because the affairs of state or municipality are not perfectly administered, nor because of the exigencies of party.

That there is much to condemn in political conduct is also true, and corruption, whether in the primaries or the Presidency, is most potent in weakening the integrity of ambitious young men. The best influences of church and school hardly serve to offset the tendency of daily contact with men who have no ideal standards of citizenship. The idea of public gain without commensurate public service is a most insidious tempter, to be resisted by every instinct of true manhood. This is not a matter of abstract speculation, but a practical condition here and now, and one that every educated man must face.

You recall the scene of Shakespeare, where Hotspur on the field of battle, "breathless and weary" after the conflict, encountered a certain lord, "perfumed like a milliner," holding to his nose a pouncet-box, and calling the soldiers, who bore the dead bodies by, untaught knaves, "to bring a slovenly, unhandsome corse betwixt the wind and his nobility." Hotspur adds: "It made me mad to see him shine so brisk, and smell so sweet, ... and tell me but for these vile guns, he would himself have been a soldier." I mean no undue disrespect to educated and refined gentlemen who stand aloof from the political field because it smells of "villainous saltpetre," and is altogether too dirty and dangerous for their respectability and ease. The intelligence of the nation should guide the nation, and any educated man who stands by and views with indifference or timidity the struggle for the triumph of the best elements of society and the best principles, deserves the objurgations of every valiant Hotspur in the land. A minister recently said: "It is as much your duty to attend the primaries as the prayer-meeting." I would have educated young men take a hand in every contest where order and justice and honesty are endangered; I would have them independently take a stand with whatever party or faction, at a given time, may represent the best cause. I would have them measure public service and public reward by the strict standard of equity; I would have them recognize the duty of active practical citizenship.

The people are keen to detect wrong aims in political life, and in their minds they speedily relegate the politician who shows himself unworthy to the plane of his motives. They as speedily recognize probity and patriotism and devotion to the commonwealth, and the truly royal men in public life are enshrined in their hearts and are made an example to their children. The majority of citizens are right in their feeling and purpose; their fault is in their apathy. Edgar W. Nye, the genial humorist, quaintly expressed a deep thought when he said: "To-day there is not a crowned head on the continent of Europe that does not recognize this great truth—viz.: that God alone, speaking through the united voices of the common people, declares the rulings of the Supreme Court of the Universe." In the long run the voice of all the people is just.

In the sixteenth century literature we find a choice bit of truth and eloquence: "Of Law there can be no less acknowledged than that her seat is the Bosom of God; her voice the harmony of the world." Moral order is a part of the beneficent law of the world; only by conformity to it can an individual or a nation prosper. If ideals of truth and right are existent in the mind of the Creator, are implanted in human nature and revealed through society, no one can escape from their authority. One of the old Sophists declared honesty to be "sublime simplicity," and those are yet found who subscribe to the creed. The life that is controlled by mere prudence is likely at some time to commit a fatal error. That State is sound that lives under the law of God, that regards principles of right and maintains healthy sentiment.

VI.

OPTIMISM AND INTEREST.

Ground and nature of interest—Many interests—Validity of instinct—Moral grades—Cultivation of interest—Happiness—Occupation.

Not long ago I met an old acquaintance, and by way of greeting asked how affairs were with him. "All right," he replied; "business is looking up; the city is improving; the State is in a better condition; we have a good Legislature, a good Governor; it is a beautiful day, a beautiful world; everything is all right." And I went on my way, meditating on interest and optimism. His interest in life was not due to any recent stroke of good fortune, but was habitual.

The optimist is your best philosopher. He adapts himself to the world and uses it. He selects the best that life offers, and, when the sky is gloomy, he lives in hope of bright days. He has faith in the ultimate beneficent outcome of the plan of the Creator. As there is light for the eye, sound for the ear, form for the touch, aromas for the smell, food for the taste, so there is an object in the outer world, adapted to every human instinct and impulse. The impulse for life and action, the desire for property, the impulse for friendship, the impulses of wonder, æsthetic admiration, and religious worship—each has its objective counterpart. Man is adjusted to his environment, and his environment includes the whole round world of utility and sentiment. Human life is perpetual activity, a searching for objects that will meet material needs and conduce to spiritual development. The feeling of interest arises when the mind finds the object of its search or feels that it is on the right track.

Interest is the condition of the mind that makes a thing of value to us. It is the cry of *Eureka* when a fitting discovery is made. It is the magnetic relation between impulse and the end at which it aims, between man and the outer world, between man and himself. It makes life worth living, and is the secret of activity and progress. Inasmuch as interest shows the kind of objects that appeal to the mind, it is a revelation of character.

The objects, which a man may cherish are limitless. He may rejoice in his strength, his personal adornment, his lands and money, his books and works of art. He may find an eager interest in his own image as pictured in the minds of his relatives, friends, or fellow citizens. He may take pride in family or in personal glory and honor. Men pose before the world; they act often with reference to the appreciation they will receive. It is told that the poet Keats could not live without applause. Carlyle says men write history, not with supreme regard for facts, but for the writing. Nero conceived that he was a musician, poet, and actor, surpassing in merit the geniuses of his age.

Man's attitude toward wisdom and religion, the quality of his thoughts and feelings, his aspirations, constitute his spiritual interest. The sentiments of his soul are his; for them he is responsible, and in them he finds satisfaction or humiliation.

As one forgets self and self-interest, more and more he makes the whole world his possession. Nature, the welfare of others, man in history and literature, the Maker of all, may become objects of regard. A French nobleman who in the vicissitudes of revolution lost his estates and titles, but received a small pension from the government, became a philosopher and had the world at his command. For slight pay, willing service for his daily needs was his; private gardens, public parks, the broad landscape, the sky were his to enjoy, and he was free from care and fear. Some interests are universal, not the heritage and possession of one, but, like sun and air, free. They fall "as the gentle rain from heaven upon the place beneath," and bless him that receives. Rich in experience is he who can see in the drifted gleaming snows on our mountain peaks more than the summer's irrigation, in the green plains of May more than the growing crops of wheat and alfalfa, in the orchard bloom more than the promise of fruit, in public education and charity more than political and social prudence, in religious devotion more than conventionality. For him blessings come on the morning breeze, gleam from the midnight sky, appear in the quality of mercy, and spring from communion with the Soul of Nature.

Prometheus is said to have given to men a portion of all the qualities possessed by the other animals—the lion, the monkey, the wolf—hence the many traits that are manifest in his complex nature. There is a slight suggestion of evolution in this—that man is but the highest stage of animal development, and that his refined emotions are but the instincts of the lower orders modified by complex groupings. We grant the process, but not necessarily the inference. An apple is none the less an apple because it is the product of an unbroken development from a germ and simple shoot. The spirit of self-sacrifice need be none the less valid because it is a late phase of some simple instinct. We believe the world was fashioned according to an intelligent plan, a plan gradually realized, and that its meaning is found, not in the lower, but in the higher stages of development. We explain the purpose of creation, not by the first struggle of a protozoan for food, but by the last aspiration of man for heaven.

"From harmony, from heavenly harmony,
This universal frame began:
From harmony to harmony
Through all the compass of the notes it ran,
The diapason closing full in Man."

The latest science hesitates to question the validity of our higher emotional life. It is becoming antiquated to say that, because we are descended from animals, our sense of duty, our feelings of faith and reverence have no more significance than the animal instincts from which they may have developed. There they are in all their refinement, need, and suggestiveness, and, as such, are a proper ground of belief. A late philosophical evolutionist says it is useless to theorize about our impulse to pray, its use or futility—we pray because we cannot help praying. Evolution is undergoing the test of the last stage of a scientific process—in this instance that of fitness to explain the facts of man's nature. It may not escape the test by denying the facts.

Pardon the seeming digression, but the reasonableness of our faith is the ground of interest. Interest vanishes with the genuineness of our supposed treasure. We do not like to handle counterfeit coin; we do not value antiquities and sacred relics of modern manufacture, or mementos that no longer represent cherished memories. Much that stimulates the higher life would perish did we doubt the truth of our nature; the glory of the world would depart were the soul lost out of it.

Some interests have sacred claims above others; there is a hierarchy amongst our impulses. Analyze the fact as we may, duty still remains. Moral laws and their practical application are progressively revealed by the relations of men in society. We may believe the laws are there in the nature of things, but that our discovery of them is gradual, as is the discovery of the unchanging laws of physics. The moral problem is the old one of the struggle between light and darkness, between good and evil, between duty and pleasure—the problem of responsibility, character, and destiny. In its modern form it is the problem of utility, that is, of life and happiness. But utilitarianism includes, and ever must include, the happiness that comes from the exercise of the higher spiritual functions, from the sense of duty performed, and from belief in divine approbation.

Interests chosen and pursued reveal the character. Men do not gather grapes of thorns nor figs of thistles. "A good tree can not bring forth evil fruit; neither can a corrupt tree bring forth good fruit." The outward act is but the visible expression of the inner life.

There is something more than a pleasing myth in the Greek conception of choosing the lot of life. Every responsible act of free will is gradually fixing our destiny. The conduct of life is not a series of skirmishes with fate; it is fate itself, and a thing largely of our own creation. We are constructing the future out of the present. For the goal that we may finally reach we are even now running the race, the direction is already chosen, and, if we find ourselves on the wrong road, time is already lost.

Times change, science brings in new conceptions, superstitions vanish, beliefs are modified, new conditions and duties arise. But as the scenes shift and new actors come on the stage, the themes are still human history, comedy, and tragedy. The argument of the play is still the triumph of heroism and the reward of virtue. The spectators still smile at innocent pleasures, weep with misfortune, and applaud sentiment and worth, and the orchestra still plays the triumph or the dirge as the curtain falls on the final scene. The ideals of the saints, the courage of heroes, the sufferings of martyrs still teach their lesson. Reverence for God, justice, benevolence, the ethical worth of the individual are still dominant ideas.

If our ideals are less severe, they are more practical; if our heroism is less phenomenal, it takes on new forms or is reserved for imperative need; if we shrink from martyrdom, it may be because martyrdom is sometimes folly; if we worship with less zeal, we are more conscious of the rational grounds of worship. Our justice and benevolence have become more useful and practical, and reach all men. The problems of physical comfort and material progress, of practical charity, of political justice, of social purity, of the rights of all classes of men, of education, of peace and good will, of the true grounds of religious faith are at the front, and claim our interest and devotion. Romance is not dead. The modern hero has his opportunity, an opportunity open as never before to all kinds and conditions of men. Every educated young man has an unlimited field, a free lance, and a cause worthy of his valor. Let him go forth, as an ideal knight of old, pure in heart and life, with consecrated sword, to aid misfortune, to defend the people, and fight bravely for truth and right.

I have seen young men going about, dallying with this or that pleasure, physically lazy, mentally indolent, morally indifferent, burdened with *ennui*, aimless, making no struggle. Will power must be awakened, life given to the mechanism, or it will go to rust and decay. While there is hope there is life. When interest is gone, the mind and spirit are dead, and the body is dying. What a hopeless lump of clay is he who, standing in this infinitely glorious world of ours and having eyes sees not, having ears hears not, and having a heart understands not.

What shall men do who have not come to a consciousness of their better impulses, to whom the number and worth of human possibilities are unknown, who have hidden, silent chords, awaiting the touch that will set them vibrating? Plainly by studying the highest types of men, the completeness of whose inner life is revealed in their deeds and thoughts. By contact with a better than himself one comes to know his better self. Under the influence of great companionship, whether in life or literature, new conceptions may appear in the vacant soul.

A popular work of fiction lately published shows incidentally how great conceptions may grow in a foreign and incongenial soil. It treats of the times of Nero and the early struggles of the Christians in Rome. Amidst that folly, profligacy, debauchery, strife, and cruelty, the Christian purity, humility, brotherly love, and faith in God are made to stand forth in world-wide contrast. Through a series of dramatic events, possessing for him a powerful interest, a Roman patrician comes to receive the Christian ideas, and, under the nurture of interest, they gradually wax strong and become the dominant impulses of his being. A fellow patrician, maintaining a persistent attitude of indifference to the new truths, lives and dies, to the last a degenerate Roman and a Stoic.

A remote interest whose attainment is doubtful may come to wholly possess the mind. A young man, misunderstood and underestimated by friends, suffering years of unrequited effort, persevering in silent determination, standing for the right, making friends with all classes, seizing strongly the given opportunity, defying popularity, and thereby winning it, may gradually rise to prominence through long years of focusing of effort.

Man's free will makes him responsible for his interests. Aristotle's dictum comes down to us in an unbroken line of royal descent: Learn to find interest in right things. Repugnance to the sternest demands of duty may be converted into liking, and, in the process, character is made. If you have a need for mathematics, science, history, poetry, or philanthropy, cultivate it, and interest will come as a benediction upon the effort. I sometimes think the gods love those who in youth are compelled to walk in hard paths. Rudyard Kipling has a trace of imperialism which is not the least valuable feature of his unique writings. In a late story he describes the transformation of a son of wealth who is already far on the road to folly—one of those nervous, high-strung lads who in the face of hardship hides behind his mother, and is a particular nuisance to all sensitive people. Crossing the ocean in a palatial steamer, he chances to roll off into the Atlantic and is conveniently hauled aboard a fishing schooner, out for a three months' trip. He has literally tumbled into a new life, where he is duly whipped into a proper frame of mind and made to earn his passage and a small wage, by sharing the hardships of the fishermen. In time he is returned to his parents, together with a bonus of newly acquired common sense and love for useful work. Hardship did for him what all his father's wealth could not buy.

It is in the time of need that men seek ultimate reality. A scientific writer, after speaking of our interest in the friendship and appreciation of men, refers to our need of friendship and appreciation in our time of stern trial, when we stand alone in the performance of duty. Then we have an intuitive consciousness of a Being supremely just and appreciative, who recognizes worth at its exact value, and will duly reward. We feel that in Him we live and move and have our being. The finite conditions of life drive us to the thought of an infinite One, who possesses in their fullness the ideals imperfectly realized in us. When the world swings from under our feet we need a hold on heaven. In these modern days we need the spirit of the hero who places honor above life, the spirit that places character above material advantage. Without it we are like Falstaff, going about asking "What is honor?" and complaining because it "hath no skill in surgery." Balzac, describing one of his human types, paints a striking picture. A miser is on his death bed. As the supreme moment approaches, and a golden crucifix is held before his face, he fixes his glazing eyes upon it with a look of miserly greed, and, with a final effort of his palsied hand, attempts to grasp it. He takes with him to the other world in his soul the gold, not the Christ crucified.

There are people who demand a series of ever varied, thrilling, fully satisfying emotional experiences. For them "the higher life consists in a sort of enthusiastic fickleness. The genius must wander like a humming-bird in the garden of divine emotions." When they do not save themselves by devotion to scholarly work or by refuge in the church, they frequently end in pessimism, madness, or suicide. They exalt the *Ego,* do not lose self in the pursuit of proper objects of utility. Nordau has done the world one service in branding them as degenerates, living in abnormal excitement, instead of employing the calm, strong, balanced use of their powers. Their fate is fittingly suggested by a choice sentence from a well-known writer, describing Byron's "Don Juan": "It is a mountain stream, plunging down dreadful chasms, singing through grand forests, and losing itself in a lifeless gray alkali desert." Goethe's Faust sets forth—be it noted, under the guidance of the devil—to find complete enjoyment, and tries the whole round of experience. Everything palls upon him, until he at last finds permanent satisfaction in earnest practical labor for the welfare of his fellow-men. In the words of Faust:

"He only earns his freedom and existence
Who daily conquers them anew."

Labor! It is the secret of happiness. We are born bundles of self-activity, in infancy ever developing our powers by ceaseless movement, with eager curiosity ever reaching out toward knowledge of external things, ever laboring and constructing in imitation of the great, working world. Unless our energies are wasted by folly and our hearts are chilled by custom, it is the natural condition, even as children, older and wiser, but still as children, ever to extend with enthusiasm the boundary of knowledge, and in reality to join in the labor which was the play-work of our childhood. And when our effort overcomes, creates, develops power, aids humanity, we are conscious of the joy of true living. In our work self must be put in the background. "He that loseth his life shall find it." The great Goethe, once weighed down with a mighty sorrow, forgot his grief in the study of a new and difficult science.

It is a mistake to suppose that interest and happiness may not attach to duty. Duty is not a dead, barren plant that no more will put forth green leaves and blossom. Philanthropists do not need our sympathy. A man of learning, culture, and ability, capable of enjoying keenly the amenities of civilization, and of winning worldly success, goes on a mission to the interior of Darkest Africa. Amid hardships and dangers, he offers his life to help an alien race in its suffering, ignorance, and savagery. He makes this devotion his supreme interest, and who shall say that his satisfaction will not be as great as that of the most favored son of wealth amid the luxuries of civilization? "He that goeth forth and weepeth, bearing precious seed, shall doubtless come again with rejoicing, bringing his sheaves with him."

One great purpose of education is to increase and strengthen our interests. It shows the many fields of labor and gives us power to work therein; it reveals the laws and beauties of the natural world; it introduces us to many lands and peoples, and acquaints us with the problems and means of progress; it opens to us the treasury of man's best thoughts; it gives us philosophical and poetic insight.

Sydney Smith, indulging one of his quaint conceits, says: "If you choose to represent the various parts in life by holes upon a table, of different shapes—some circular, some triangular, some square, some oblong—and the persons acting these parts by bits of wood of similar shapes, we shall generally find that the triangular person has got into the square hole, the oblong into the triangular, and a square person has squeezed himself into the round hole." This fancy has some truth, but more of nonsense. "Men at some time are masters of their fates." Create your place in life and fill it, or adapt yourself to the best place you can find. The choice of occupation is important, but filling well the profession chosen is more important. Turn your knowledge and power to the performance of to-day's duty.

Lowell in his "Vision of Sir Launfal" imparts one of the sweetest lessons man may learn. Sir Launfal is to set forth on the morrow in search of the Holy Grail, the cup used by our Saviour at the last supper, and in his sleep there comes to him a true vision. As in his dream he rides forth with pride of heart, at his castle gate a leper begs alms, and in scorn he tosses him a piece of gold. Years of fruitless search pass, and as he returns old, broken, poor, and homeless, he again meets the leper at the castle gate, and in Christ's name he offers a cup of water. And lo! the leper stands forth as the Son of God, and proclaims the Holy Grail is found in the wooden cup shared with communion of heart. The morn came and Sir Launfal hung up his idle armor. He had found the object of his quest in the humble duty at hand.

A poet of our day quaintly but not irreverently writes of the future life, "When the Master of all Good Workmen shall set us to work anew." There we shall work for the joy of it; there we shall know things in their reality; there we shall enjoy the perfect appreciation of the Master, and know the blessedness of labor performed in His service. Thus the lesson is good for this world as well as the next.

"And only the Master shall praise us, and only the Master shall blame;
And no one shall work for money, and no one shall work for fame;
But each for the joy of the working, and each, in his separate star,
Shall draw the Thing as he sees It for the God of Things as They Are."

VII.

THE ETHICAL AND ÆSTHETIC ELEMENTS IN EDUCATION.

Baccalaureate Day—Courage and opportunity—"Laughter of the soul at itself,"—Attitude toward religion—Love of art.

A historic sentiment is associated with the laurel tree, sacred to Apollo; with the laurel wreath which crowned the victor in the Pythian games, was the emblem of the poet, rested upon the heads of victorious generals, later indicated academic honors, and has become a figure of speech and a gem in poetic literature. The Baccalaureate Day—the day when victors in the endeavor to reach the graduate's goal figuratively are crowned with the fruited laurel—we would preserve. We would preserve it for its history, its significance, its associations, its sentiments, its memories, its promise, and its religious suggestion. We would preserve it, not only to celebrate scholastic honors already won, but as a fitting occasion to consider some of those deeper lessons whose meaning will appear through experience in the School of Life.

*   *   *   *   *

Higher education ever enlarges the borders of science and leads forth into new fields. It transmutes superstition into knowledge. It is the spirit of civilization and the leader of progress. It stands at the summit of human development, represents the aggregate of human knowledge, is the goal for intellectual endeavor, and it points the way for the discovery and progress of the future.

There was a time when many scholars turned the pages of literature, in which were preserved the deeds, investigations, and thoughts of men, solely that they might develop and enjoy their own powers; when they devoted themselves to Truth for its own sake; when they stood isolated, as in a world of their own, considering naught but their own welfare and, perhaps, their relation to their Maker. Men dwelt in caves, in remote deserts, or within gloomy walls to dwarf the bodily and worldly impulses and to rise to a serene contemplation of God and His truths, disregarding the appeal of ignorant or suffering humanity and the duty of adding works to faith.

Our relations to our fellow-men give rise to nearly the entire Ethical Code. Society cares for us, educates us, develops us, and it has claims upon us, not on purely selfish or utilitarian grounds, but under a higher ethical idea, whose sanction is the perfection and will of God. The law of God requires effort for humanity, government enjoins it, charity demands it. The Associationist, the Utilitarian, and the Evolutionist teach it.

An honorable character and a useful life are full of influence. And there are hundreds of ways, in some of which, without burdensome effort, one may be a blessing to others. Ignorance may be awakened to its condition, vice may be shamed, sorrow may be assuaged, fear may be changed into hope, sloth may be aroused to action, doubt may be converted into faith.

Go forth and join in the labor you are fitted for. If you have a truth, utter it; if you have had superior privileges, impart to others; if you have an insight into principles of conduct, stand for them; if you have a trained eye and a deft hand, use your skill. Externalize the powers of your being; find outward expression for your inward thought.

Thank God for a courageous man, a true Anglo-Saxon man, a man whose convictions are deeply rooted, and who guards them as his very life. Heroes, philanthropists, and martyrs are his exemplars. He has a work to do, and he enters upon it as his fathers battled for the right. The sensualist, the dreamer, and the fatalist lie supine, are lulled by the summer breeze, and gaze upon the drifting panorama of clouds with playful imagination. The man of duty marches forth and takes the fixed stars for his guide.

The educated young man of to-day has every reason to thank the stars under which he was born. Behind him is the teaching of the civilized world—the poetry and art of Greece, the laws and institutions of Rome, the growth of Christianity, the Mediæval commingling of forces and evolution of rare products, the Renaissance, the religious and political emancipation, invention, science, art, poetry, and philosophy. Behind him is the history of the Anglo-Saxon race, its courage and deeds of valor, its profound earnestness, its stern ideals. Behind him is Puritan New England and liberty. Around him lies the new land of promise with its natural blessings of air, sun, mountains, and plains, with its mineral wealth and industrial possibility, with its people of pride, energy, intelligence, and high enthusiasm. Before him lie the development of a great and unique civilization, a wonder of material progress, a rare growth of poetic power and free spirit under new and fostering conditions. Before the youth of this State is the possibility of success in any pursuit, of rise to influence, of contributing to the formative period of a new commonwealth. There is every inducement to be a courageous, energetic, and ideal man. Those who have made our history, most of them, are still living, but their work is nearly accomplished, and you will take up the responsibility. May our great system of public instruction contribute to fill the State in coming decades with noble men and women who are not afraid of ideals.

* * * * *

Man may deceive others, but is shamed at the tribunal of his own better judgment. A celebrated lecturer describes what he calls the "Laughter of the Soul at Itself," "a laughter that it rarely hears more than once without hearing it forever." He says: "You would call me a partisan if I were to describe an internal burst of laughter of conscience at the soul. Therefore let Shakespeare, let Richter, let Victor

Hugo, let cool secular history put before us the facts of human nature." We may refer to one illustration: Jean Valjean, one of Hugo's characters, an escaped and reformed convict, was about to see an innocent man condemned for his own act, through mistaken identity. He tried to make himself believe self-preservation was justifiable, and as the mental struggle between Self and Duty went on he seemed to hear a voice: "Make yourself a mask if you please; but, although man sees your mask, God will see your face; although your neighbors see your life, God will see your conscience." And again came the internal burst of laughter. The author proceeds: "Valjean finally confessed his identity; and the court and audience, when he uttered the words, 'I am Jean Valjean,' 'felt dazzled in their hearts, and that a great light was shining before them.'"

* * * * *

Science does away with superstition and many an error, it makes known the laws of nature, it applies them to practical ends, it is the handmaid of civilization, it emphasizes the welfare of humanity, it shows the working of the mechanism within the field of demonstrative knowledge, the finite, knowable land of the real. Science exceeds its purpose only whenever it proclaims that there is no field of spiritual knowledge, glimpses of which may be seen by souls that dwell upon the heights. Some would measure the earth with a carpenter's rule, forgetting Him "Who hath measured the waters in the hollow of His hand, and meted out Heaven with the span, and comprehended the dust of the earth in a measure, and weighed the mountains in scales, and the hills in a balance."

Carlyle says: "Religion in most countries is no longer what it was, and should be—a thousand-voiced psalm from the heart of man to the invisible Father, the fountain of all goodness, beauty, truth, and revealed in every revelation of these; but for the most part a wise, prudential feeling, grounded on mere calculation, a matter, as all others now are, of expediency and utility; whereby some smaller quantum of earthly enjoyment may be exchanged for a larger quantum of celestial enjoyment." But again and more truly he says: "Religion cannot pass away. The burning of a little straw may hide the stars of the sky, but the stars are there and will reappear."

Once a pupil asked to be excused from exercises in which choice extracts from the Bible were sometimes read, simply because they were from the Bible; but he listened with pleasure to good thoughts from other books, though these books contained many a palpable error. Aside from the view which makes the Bible the Sacred Book of the Christian believer, he had not thought of its value to a large portion of the human race. He had not regarded it in the light of history and philosophy. The ideals for which the Hebrew race has stood, the wonderful prophecies of great and far-seeing men, the grand poems of faith and promise, the words of condensed wisdom, the maxims for right living, the Beatitudes, the teaching of the Parables, the spirit of adoration, the moral code, the allegorical wisdom never had been contemplated apart from the religious view, against which he had imbibed a prejudice.

Permit me to speak from the standpoint of history and philosophy. The Christian religion is a chief source of our peculiar civilization, of the character of our institutions, of the growth of altruism, of the equality of man, of the supreme worth of the inner motive, of charity, of liberty. It has given the world the highest examples of pure and devoted lives.

I have a friend who is struck with the tale of how Buddha, wearing a Brahman's form, when "drought withered all the land," encountered a starving tigress with her cubs, and, in the unbounded pity of his heart, offered himself a sacrifice to their hunger. He says: "Here is a beautiful religion for me." And yet he is not touched by the story of a Saviour who carried the burden of the pains and sorrows of many and died that they might live.

Disregard no good, wherever found. The human race must have its ideals. Thousands have felt what a famous man has expressed, that, were there no religion, men would of necessity invent it and worship a false idea. The religion of Mohammed is better than the idolatry of the Arab; the idolatry of the Arab was better than nothing. The races—each at its own stage—have been improved by their religions. The Scandinavian conception of Walhalla; the Ancient Oracle at Dodona, where the priests in gloomy groves caught the responses of Zeus from the whisperings of the sacred oaks; the ancestor worship of the Chinese, the system of symbolism in Egypt—all represented the struggle toward ideal life and the notion of retributive justice. With bowed head and reverential heart I would stand in the presence of any sincere devotion, the uplifting of the soul in prayer to the God of its faith; how much more in the presence of that worship which the best intelligence of the best races has accepted. And how often one misinterprets the real meaning of an alien religion. The "Light of Asia" gives a meaning to Nirvana never heard from the pulpit:

> "Foregoing self, the Universe grows 'I';
> If any teach NIRVANA is to cease,
> Say unto such they lie."

Let young men learn as a common-sense proposition that, though creeds may change, though there may be frequent readjustments of theological beliefs, the religious sentiment is an essential fact of our nature, and has a meaning the depth of which they have not sounded.

* * * * *

The love of Art is necessary to the complete man. Whatever may be said of the cold, intellectual spirit, one attains a high standard of humanity only when he possesses a heart warmed and ennobled by a vivid conception of the Beautiful found in the rainbow, the color of the leaf, and the sparkle of the rill, works framed in nature and hung in God's great art gallery—the universe. Man sees the real spirit shining through material forms, and architecture, sculpture, painting, music, and poetry follow. Noble thought and action, right and truth, all perfect things partake of the essence of Beauty. Art adds to nature; it casts a halo:

> "The light that never was on sea or land,
> The consecration and the Poet's dream."

I have often dwelt upon the lines of Wordsworth:

> "To me the meanest flower that blows can give
> Thoughts that do often lie too deep for tears."

I have often wished to hear a sermon arguing from this thought the existence of God and the immortality of the soul. The peculiar nature of the soul, that transmutes sensation into divine emotion—a sweetness, longing, and reverence that are not of earth—is it not suggestive of all that is claimed by religious faith? Wordsworth rightly ascribed a dwarfed nature to him who sees only meaningless form and dull color in the flower:

> "A primrose by a river's brim
> A yellow primrose was to him,
> And it was nothing more."

That education is inadequate which ignores the value of man's æsthetic nature and neglects its growth.

VIII.

PROGRESS AS REALIZATION.

Theme illustrated—Individual history—Ideals and development—Significance of higher emotional life—Future of history and philosophy—Realization.

"For now we see through a glass, darkly."

"Yet I doubt not through the ages one increasing purpose runs,
And the thoughts of men are widened with the process of the suns."

In the process of development nature goes from potentiality to higher and higher actuality; what is in its being as tendency becomes real. We may not suppose the movement that of spontaneous energy toward accidental results, but rather the progressive realization of what is in the entire rational scheme of the universe.

From the nebular mass sprang worlds and suns greater and less, substance and form in infinite variety, plant life in progressive orders, animal life in ascending types. Conscious existence gradually became responsive to the multitude of nature's impressions. The broken rays of light displayed their rainbow hues to the growing power and delicacy of the eye; sound revealed its keys, qualities, and harmonies to the increasing susceptibility of the ear. Mind, as it developed, realized in its consciousness new laws and ever greater wonders of the outer world. On the objective side the laws were, the tinted sky and the murmuring stream were, before mind became cognizant of them in their perfection and beauty. Any serious contemplation of the great law of development, in its full meaning, should inspire hope and purpose in life. It suggests, not only sublime fulfilment for the world, but large possibility for the individual man. The natural world, plants, animals, the human race, institutions, science, art, religion, all animate individual beings, man as an individual, have their history of development, which suggests its lesson.

Nature is aspiration. From chaos to the world of this geologic age, from protoplasm to man, from savagery to civilization, from ignorance to culture, from symbolism to developed art, from egoism to altruism, from germ to fruit, from infancy to maturity, from realization to higher realization, has been the process. And this plan seems the only one adapted to satisfy the nature and thought of rational being. A world perfected, all possibilities realized, no chance for higher attainment—these are conditions of monotony and death. The old Heraclitus was right when he proclaimed the principle of the world to be a *becoming*.

The child's history, in a way, is an epitome of the history of the race. At first he is deaf and blind to the world of objects. Note how the possibilities of his being become realities, how knowledge grows in variety and definiteness, until the external world stands revealed, each object in its place, each event in its order, until notions of time, space, cause, and right rise into consciousness. The child is father of the man in the sense that the man can become only what he was implicitly in childhood.

There is a tale of Greek mythology that Minerva sprang full-grown from the head of Jove—a perfect being. We would rather contemplate a being with possibilities not completely revealed. A philosopher said that if Truth were a bird which he had caught and held in his hand he would let it escape for the pleasure of renewed pursuit. There are the wonders of nature and of physical evolution; but transcendently great are the wonders of mind, and the view of its possibilities of endless development—a thing that we believe will live on, when the sun, moon, and stars shall be darkened.

The educated young man of to-day is the heir of the ages. All that science, art, literature, philosophy, civilization have achieved is his. All that thought has realized through ages of slow progress, all that has been learned through the mistakes made in the dim light of the dawn of human history, all that has been wrought out through devotion, struggle, and suffering, he may realize by the process of individual education. The law of progress still holds for the race and for him. He is a free factor, with a duty to help realize still more of the promise of human existence.

"Know thyself" was a wonderful maxim of the ancient philosopher, and it leads to knowledge. "Know thy powers" is a better maxim for practice, and it is a fault that men regard their limitations and not their capabilities. We look with contempt upon a lower stage of our own growth. Not for the world would we lose a little from our highest attainment. The view is relative, and we have but to advance our position and life is subject to new interpretation.

This is a period of the fading out of old ideals as they merge into higher ones not yet clearly defined. The reverence for nature, for its symbolism, the sanctions of religion, the transcendental belief, the poetic insight have somewhat fallen away, and the world is partly barren because not yet rehabilitated. Ideals are regarded as fit for schoolgirl essays, for weakly sentimentality, for dreamers, for those who do not understand the meaning of the new science and the new civilization. Ideals! The transcendent importance of ideals is just appearing. Not an invention could be made, not a temple could be built, not a scheme for the improvement of government and society could be constructed, not a poem or a painting could be executed, not an instance of progress could occur without ideals. The world may be conceived as an ideal, the development of all things is toward ideals. We are at a stage of that development; the progression is infinite, ever toward perfection, toward God, the Supreme Good. Lamartine said wisely: "The ideal is only truth at a distance."

Do circumstances forbid the possibility of higher development? Then let the individual, in a chosen vocation, however humble, lose himself in obedience and devotion to it, and thus, as a hero, live to his own well-being and the welfare of others. Thereby he will find blessedness. Carlyle's "Everlasting Yea" shows this passage: "The Situation that has not its Duty, its Ideal, was never yet occupied by man. Yes, here, in this poor, miserable, hampered, despicable actual, wherein thou even now standest, here or nowhere is thy Ideal; work it out therefrom; and working, believe, live, be free. Fool! the Ideal is in thyself, the impediment, too, is in thyself; thy Condition is but the stuff thou art to shape that same Ideal out of; what matters whether such stuff be of this sort or that, so the Form thou give it be heroic, be poetic? O thou that pinest in the imprisonment of the Actual and criest bitterly to the gods for a kingdom wherein to rule and create, know this of a truth: the thing thou seekest is already with thee, here or nowhere, couldst thou only see!"

Here is a striking story, related as true: A young man had met with misfortune, accident, and disease, and was suffering from a third paralytic stroke. He had lost the use of his voice, of his limbs, and of one arm. A friend visited him one day and asked how he was. He reached for his tablet and wrote: "All right, and bigger than anything that can happen to me." By energy of will, by slowly increasing physical and mental exercise, he reconquered the use of his body and mind—gradually compelled the dormant nerve centres to awake and resume their functions. Later he wrote: "The great lesson it taught me is that man is meant to be, and ought to be, stronger and more than anything that can happen to him. Circumstances, fate, luck are all outside, and, if we cannot always change them, we can always beat them. If I couldn't have what I wanted, I decided to want what I had, and that simple philosophy saved me."

A healthy philosophy, speculative or common sense, a healthy ethics, theoretical or practical, are indispensable to youth. Away with unfree will, and pessimism, and pleasure philosophy, and the notion of a perfected world and a goal attained. Substitute therefor vigorous freedom, cheerful faith and hope, right and duty, and belief in development. Most of the great poets and artists, most of the successful business men have struggled with difficulties, and have wrought out of their conditions their success. Burns did not permit poverty, obscurity, lack of funds, lack of patronage, lack of time to destroy or weaken the impulse of his genius. Shakespeare (if this poet-king be not indeed dethroned by logic) with but imperfect implements of his craft wrought heroically, and realized the highest possibilities of literary creation. The biography of success is filled with the names of men in a sense self-made.

Education is the unfolding of our powers. There is the realm of knowledge: the relations of number and space, as revealed to a Laplace or a Newton; the discoveries and interpretations of science, as they appear to a Tyndall or a Spencer; history, in whose light alone we can fully interpret any subject of knowledge; literature, whose pages glow with the best thought and feeling of mankind; philosophy and religious truth, with their grasp of the meaning of life; art, that is a divine revelation in material form—all that has been realized in the consciousness of man. The race has taken ages to attain the present standard of civilization and enlightenment. The life of the individual attains it through education. With some distinction of native tendencies, education makes the difference between the Dahoman and the Bostonian. Tennyson, in his "Locksley Hall," in a mood of disappointment and pessimism, would seek the land of palms, of savagery and ignorance, and abjure the "march of Mind" and "thoughts that shake mankind;" but a healthful reaction arouses again his better impulse, and he counts "the *gray* barbarian lower than the Christian *child*."

Every young man who aims at medicine, theology, law, or teaching, who aims at the best development of his powers, needs all the education he can gain before he enters upon independent labor. All need a broad foundation of general knowledge upon which to rear the structure of special knowledge and skill. Our grandfathers got along with the grammar school, the academy, college, and apprentice system; we need the high school, the graduate school, and the professional school. Men go into the field of labor without map, implements, or skill, and then wonder why they do not succeed. The generation has advanced; more is known, more is demanded, and undeveloped thought and skill soon find their limitations in the practical world.

We are called upon not only to feel, but to act; not merely to know, but to impart. The inner life is to realize itself in the outer world of action. Ideals are to be followed closely by deeds. A mere recluse is not in harmony with the times.

There is a thought in the following passage from Goethe not inappropriate in this place:

> "Wouldst thou win desires unbounded?
> Yonder see the glory burn!
> Lightly is thy life surrounded—
> Sleep's a shell, to break and spurn!
> When the crowd sways, unbelieving,
> Show the daring will that warms!
> He is crowned with all achieving
> Who perceives and then performs."

The child does not at first discriminate colors, but later realizes distinctions permanently existent. The child does not at first realize the force of the abstract idea of right; but, when the idea appears, it is not so much an evolution as a realization in the process of evolution of the child's consciousness. In the development of life on the earth a time came when human beings realized the existence and obligation of right as a new idea to them, not one "compounded of many simples." However produced, we may suppose that when it appears it is a unique thing, a binding and divine thing, a thing carrying with it all the implications of the Kantian philosophy—God, Freedom, and Immortality.

How religion, philosophy, ethics, maxims of experience, dictates of prudence proclaim to the ear of the youth the necessity of realizing in idea and practice a progressive, upward tendency of character! Vice is not a realization, but degeneration. Vice paralyzes the will, paralyzes the intellect, paralyzes the finer emotions, paralyzes the body, deadens the conscience to all that is positive and worthy. Men often regard only the larger duties, but character is often made by the sum of little duties performed. We are ready to use great opportunities only when we have trained our powers by diligent performance of humble work. Carlyle says: "*Do the Duty which lies nearest thee*, which thou knowest to be a Duty! Thy second Duty will already have become clearer."

It broadens our view of religion to hold that the divine impulse works in all men, and leads them toward truth; that no age or people has been left in utter darkness; that there is something common to all religions; and that in time God's full revelation will come to all nations.

"Whoe'er aspires unweariedly
Is not beyond redeeming."

May we not ask if the experience distinctively called Christian is not an actuality, the highest blossom of religious growth—if it is not a realization possible for all, if it is not an ideal sweetly, nay, transcendently, inviting? One who has read the following lines from Goethe will never forget them; he has had a glimpse of the Holy of Holies:

"Once Heavenly Love sent down a burning kiss
Upon my brow, in Sabbath silence holy;
And, filled with mystic presage, chimed the church bell slowly,
And prayer dissolved me in a fervent bliss,—
A sweet, uncomprehended yearning
Drove forth my feet through woods and meadows free,
And while a thousand tears were burning,
I felt a world arise for me."

I sat on the veranda at my home at the close of a beautiful day. The western glow was fading into a faint rose color. The pine trees on the neighboring mountain top stood out in magnified distinctness against the bright background. A bird in a near tree sang its good-night song. Just over the mountain peak a star shone out like a diamond set in pale gold. The great earth silently turned and hid the star behind the pines. The ragged outline of mountains loomed up with weird effect. The breeze freshened and waved the branches of the elms gracefully in broader curves; it seemed to come down from the heights as if with a message. It was a time for meditation. My thoughts turned for a hundredth time to the significance of the higher emotional effects in the presence of natural beauty and sublimity, and in the contemplation of exalted æsthetic and ethical conceptions.

When the hand of nature touches the chords of the human heart, may we not believe that the hand and the harp are of divine origin, and that the music produced is heavenly? I mean that the human soul with all its refinement of emotion is not material, but spiritual and Godlike; that it has written upon it a sacred message, an assurance not of earth that its destiny is boundless in time and possibility—a message profound in its meaning as the unsearchable depth of God's being.

All human institutions are progressive. Each stage of civilization is complete in itself, but preparatory to another and higher stage. Liberty, the art idea, the religious idea develop more and more as men realize in consciousness higher truths and standards. From the art that found expression in the cromlechs of the Druids to the highest embodiment of spiritual ideas, from crude faith to philosophic and religious insight, from rude mechanism to magnificence of structure and invention—such has been history, such, we believe, will be history. No wonder Carlyle exclaims: "Is not man's history and men's history a perpetual Evangel?"—an announcement of glad tidings?

It is in this philosophy that the hope of the solution of many present problems is found. In mediæval times the feudal system was the reconciliation of the opposing interests of men in a unity of service and protection. Later new conflicts arose which resulted in freedom for all classes. To-day opposition has grown from the selfish interests of capital and labor, and we believe the reconciliation will be found in a unity which will equitably combine the interests of both. Change is the law. The phœnix, ever rising from its own ashes, is stronger in pinion and more daring in flight.

Plato held to the doctrine of ideas, of eternal verities, the archetypes of all forms of existence, and believed growth in wisdom to be a gradual realization of these ideas in consciousness. Modern Platonism makes man a part of the Divine Being, with power to progress in knowledge of truth and in moral insight. This progress aims at an ultimate end that is both a realization and a reward. This view explains our nature and aspirations, our intuitive notions and sense of right; it explains the seeming providence that runs through history and makes all things work together for good; it explains that harmony of the soul with nature that constitutes divine music; it explains the insight of the poet and the faith of man. Any new theory must be a continuation of the past instead of standing in contradiction to it, must reveal the deeper meaning of old truth. The spiritual truths that belong to the history of man must be included in the new philosophy. Theories must explain in accordance with common sense, and make harmony, not discord, in our intellectual, æsthetic, and moral feelings.

"For we know in part, and we prophesy in part.

"But when that which is perfect is come, then that which is in part shall be done away.

"For now we see through a glass, darkly; but then face to face: now I know in part; but then shall I know even as also I am known."

> "Still, through our paltry stir and strife,
> Glows down the wished Ideal,
> And Longing moulds in clay what Life
> Carves in the marble Real;
> To let the new life in, we know,
> Desire must ope the portal;—
> Perhaps the longing to be so

Helps make the soul immortal.

"Longing is God's fresh heavenward will
With our poor earthward striving;
We quench it that we may be still
Content with merely living:
But would we learn that heart's full scope
Which we are hourly wronging,
Our lives must climb from hope to hope
And realize our longing."

Printed by Libri Plureos GmbH in Hamburg,
Germany